W9-BFZ-068

IT HAPPENED IN
KENTUCKY

Mimi O'Malley

TWODOT®

GUILFORD, CONNECTICUT
HELENA, MONTANA
AN IMPRINT OF THE GLOBE PEQUOT PRESS

To my husband, Mike, and John and Kate.

A · TWODOT® · BOOK

Text design: Nancy Freeborn
Map by M. A. Dubé © Morris Book Publishing, LLC

Front cover photo courtesy of Library of Congress Prints & Photographs Division, LC-DIG-nclc-00557, Women Worming Tobacco, Nicholas County.
Back cover photo courtesy of Library of Congress Prints & Photographs Division, LC-USZ62-64952, Consumptive's Room, Mammoth Cave, Kentucky.

Library of Congress Cataloging-in-Publication Data
O'Malley, Mimi.
  It happened in Kentucky / Mimi O'Malley. — 1st ed.
    p. cm. — (It happened in series)
  Includes bibliographical references and index.
  ISBN-13: 978-0-7627-3853-3
  ISBN-10: 0-7627-3853-7
  1. Kentucky—History—Anecdotes. I. Title. II. Series.
  F451.6.O43 2006
  976.9—dc22
                                        2006005042

Manufactured in the United States of America
First Edition/First Printing

CONTENTS

CONTENTS

PREFACE

I hope you enjoy reading *It Happened in Kentucky*, which chronicles some of the extraordinary people and little-known events that shaped Kentucky state history. Starting with fossil discoveries at Big Bone Lick, Kentucky played a significant role in American history and was central to the westward movement of the pioneers, who followed along the Appalachian mountain valleys and the Ohio, Mississippi, and Cumberland River valley corridors.

Although this book is not a comprehensive history of the state, every chapter offers a glimpse into an event that shaped Kentucky and its current generation of Kentuckians. Whether popular reading or classroom instruction, it is the author's intention that *It Happened in Kentucky* warms the heart and gives readers of all generations a greater appreciation of the Bluegrass State's rich history.

I am grateful to Lois Tucker and Charles Brown of the Sullivan University Library & Learning Resource Center; Sue Wight and the Genealogy staff at the Louisville Free Public Library; Adrienne Stevens of the University of Kentucky's Margaret I. King Library of Special Collections & Archives; Deacon Gus Cooper of Holy Rosary Catholic Church in Springfield, Kentucky; and Laurie Smith, City Clerk of Springfield, Kentucky.

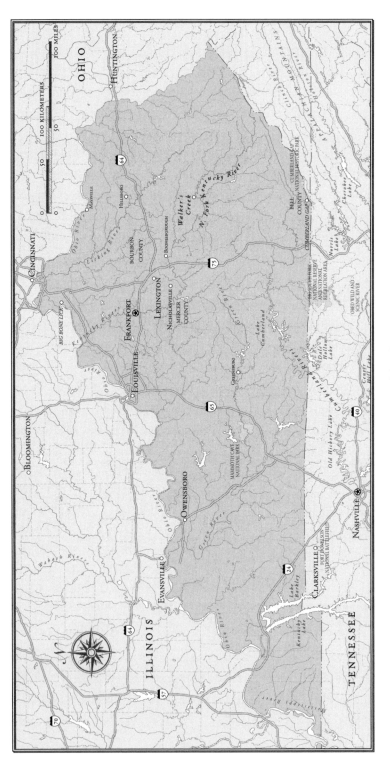

KENTUCKY

DISCOVERY OF A
MASTODON GRAVEYARD

- 1729 -

Big Bone Creek

IN THE EARLY TO MID 1700S, BRITISH SOLDIERS WERE busy claiming land and colonizing the New World for the crown. Much to their chagrin, the French army was occupied in much the same way—gaining land for France and thus limiting the land holdings of the British. In 1729, French Canadian explorer Baron de Longueuil led 440 soldiers south to begin a military assault against the Chickasaw Indians, who endangered the lines of communication between Louisiana and Canada. Along the way, the party camped along Big Bone Creek's three out-flowing springs.

While some of the soldiers were setting up camp, a small group of men explored the area, in part out of curiosity and in part to see if they could find any game animals near the low-lying marshland. Some of the soldiers stumbled upon what they thought must be animal bones. The bones were so large, however, that the men doubted they could be from an animal any of them had seen before. As they worked to dig the bones out of the soft mud, they began casting worried glances over their shoulders, wondering what kind of beasts inhabited this new territory. After more than an hour of digging, the men were left staring, their mouths agape, at several gigantic bones resembling the thigh and tusk of a large animal. Indian guides led French soldiers further along a buffalo trail at the river's edge. The riverbank was rich with more primitive bones, bleached a startling white from exposure to the sun. The group discovered teeth that weighed 10 pounds and had a diameter of 5 to 7 inches. Their bounty was truly amazing. They discovered tusks measuring 11 feet in length and 6 to 7 inches in diameter, as well as thighbones that were 5 feet long.

Although Baron de Longueuil left no official record of his men's discovery, one of his surveyors, Gaspard Chaussegros de Lery, included the site on his compass survey of the Ohio River. Longueuil did, however, ship his discoveries, which at that time were believed to be elephant bones, back to France, where they were housed in King Louis XV's two-room collection of curiosities, the Musee National d'Histoire Naturelle.

As settlers, traders, and peddlers ventured into the area, remains from this primitive graveyard began to trickle back to the American colonies, crossing the Atlantic Ocean and landing in the laboratories of Europe's leading scientists. France recognized Big Bone on its maps as early as 1744 after French cartographer Jacques Nicholas Bellin published his official map of the Louisiana Territory. On the map, Big Bone is identified as "the place where elephant bones were found in 1729."

While the French explorers of the eighteenth century were left to speculate about the animals that left behind their enormous bones, today's scientists have explained the mystery. Approximately

1.2 million years ago, three glaciers carved out the interior Ohio Valley, creating a path for the Ohio River. As the oldest glacier, the "Nebraskan," receded, it left behind flat plateaus on top of rolling valleys in northern Kentucky. The Illinois and Wisconsin glaciers subsequently left behind moraines or piles of glacial debris. Scientists theorized that the ice of the latter two glaciers became so thick that a large percentage of the earth's water became part of the glaciers and caused ocean levels to plummet significantly. Seawater trapped in the sediments left behind saline springs. This glacial recession exposed a 50-mile wide land bridge between Asia and North America through which mastodons, mammals, and other prehistoric animals traveled.

Kentucky's climate approximately 12,000 to 20,000 years ago was cool and moist, averaging about 15 to 30 degrees Fahrenheit. This climate proved to be a perfect breeding ground for mastodon, bison, musk ox, megalonyx, mylodon, stag moose, and other large game animals that came there to lick the salt left behind by the receding saltwater glaciers and to drink the water in the area. The gargantuan weight of some of these animals, perhaps weighing in excess of 11,000 pounds, caused them to sink into the swampy salt marshes. The more the animals struggled, the further they sank in the soft earth. Ultimately, many prehistoric animals died as they struggled to escape the swampy ground, becoming permanently buried and preserved in Big Bone Lick.

Eventually, the earth's climate began to warm, and the glaciers that covered vast parts of what is now North America began to melt and recede. Over time, humans began to follow the animals that migrated through the region, and the Ohio River Valley became a popular hunting site for the Paleo Indians who lived there between 8,000–10,000 B.C. The same swampy conditions that had claimed the lives of struggling mastodons helped these early people, who took advantage of the sifting mud, to ambush unsuspecting large animals.

Further expeditions to Big Bone Lick included explorer Christopher Gist's exploration in 1750 and British Colonel George Croghan's expedition in 1765. In 1807, Thomas Jefferson summoned William Clark to conduct an expedition to the site in which he yielded 300 specimens. Jefferson was anxious to discredit the European notion that degenerative animals or human giants savagely lurked among the American frontier. Subsequent explorations to Big Bone Lick failed to produce anything substantial since the area was fairly well picked dry.

Very few of the fossils collected at Big Bone Lick remain in Kentucky. Some of them are housed at the Academy of Natural Sciences in Philadelphia, the University of Nebraska, the University of Groningen (Netherlands), and Thomas Jefferson's Monticello. Excavations during the 1960s by the University of Nebraska yielded human artifacts, livestock, and wildlife fossils shedding insight into prehistoric settlement. Ice Age Pleistocene animal remains unearthed include the American mastodon, mammoth, Harlan's musk-ox, stag moose, ground sloth, extinct bison, extinct horse, deer, and caribou. By 2002, the U.S. National Park Service recognized Big Bone Lick as part of the Lewis & Clark National Historic Trail.

THE EXPEDITION OF
DR. THOMAS WALKER

- 1750 -

Cumberland Gap

ON MARCH 6, 1750, THOMAS WALKER OF Albemarle County, Virginia, left his large estate and comfortable home, Castle Hill, to lead an expedition into uncharted Kentucky territory. Accompanied by five other hardy souls—Ambrose Powell, William Tomlinson, Colby Chew, Henry Lawliss, and John Hughs—the six men explored much of the new land thirty years before Daniel Boone arrived on the scene. Not knowing what to expect or how long they would be gone, each man rode his own horse and led two packhorses that were strapped with supplies. A few hounds trailed along behind.

The lure of one's own land, the adventure of exploration, and the possibility of wealth from land speculation led many to wander from their homes and to map new territory. Thomas Walker was no exception. Walker had completed his medical studies at the College of

William and Mary and maintained a medical practice in Fredericks-burg, Virginia. However, he was captivated with the idea of land speculation and exploration. His marriage to a wealthy widow, Mil-dred Thornton Meriwether, gave him control of the 15,000-acre Cas-tle Hill estate. Following the practice of many landed gentry, Walker learned surveying so he could subdivide his estate. This surveying skill and his adventurous nature led to his 1750 expedition and his interest in land speculation.

It was these interests that led Walker, Peter Jefferson (father of President Thomas Jefferson), Joshua Fry, John Lewis, and several Meriwethers to found the Loyal Land Company in 1748. That same year, Walker accompanied Colonel James Patton from the Virginia Council, (the upper house of Virginia's legislative colonial govern-ment) as far west as the Clinch River to survey a 100,000-acre land grant. The success of that survey, along with Walker's personal con-nections and frontier experience, led to his appointment by the Loyal Land Company as an agent to lead an exploratory party westward in the spring of 1750.

During these years, the British government initiated an aggres-sive campaign of western exploration of Virginia to thwart any French land claims beyond the Alleghenies. Beginning in 1748, the Ohio Land and Loyal Land companies received royal charters to cre-ate settlements on English land claims along the Ohio River, its upper tributaries, and southwestern Virginia. Between 1750 and 1800, land was granted for as little as $20 for 100 acres, a promising opportunity for any enterprising pioneer. But much of the land was uncharted, and expeditions into the frontier had to be mounted to explore the region's possibilities.

And so it was that Thomas Walker and his friends found them-selves heading into new territory on March 7, 1750, surveying the area to see if it was hospitable for future pioneer settlements. After spending the night in Albemarle County, Virginia, Walker discussed the proposed route with Colonel Joshua Fry who had just completed a survey along the route the previous year. The party set out, following a southwesterly course and entering Buford's Gap east of the Blue Ridge Mountains.

Heavy spring rains and storms plagued the group from the beginning. River crossings were hazardous, and time spent searching for lost horses slowed the group down. Despite delays, they continued west, crossing the New River at Horseshoe fork on March 16. There they encountered a religious sect known as the Dunkards. This group had rejected other religious denominations and had forbidden voting, serving in militias, or baptizing children. However, they proved to be hospitable to the Walker party, allowing them to rest from their hard journey. After a few days, the expedition pressed forward into the Holston Valley.

Travel was tedious and cumbersome, and the party averaged only seven to eight miles per day. By March 24, the group eventually found adventurer Samuel Stalnaker, whose Virginia residence was thought to be at the western edge of civilization. Walker hoped Stalnaker would join their expedition as a guide, but Stalnaker declined. Nonetheless, the Walker party helped erect Stalnaker's cabin and, in return, Stalnaker gave Walker directions to a place called Cave Gap. The Clinch River and Cave Gap were frequently traveled paths known to adventurers traveling west. Based on conversations with others, it seemed Stalnaker was either personally acquainted or familiar with Cave Gap. After resting a few days at the Stalnaker site, the Walker party set a northwest course past the Clinch Mountains and Clinch River.

Traveling did not become easier. Fallen trees, copperhead snakes, and rattlesnakes hampered the group's journey. As they approached Powell Mountain Valley, they came upon two accessible passes. One was where the Shawnee River cut its way through the mountain range. They chose the other, a well-worn pass used by Indians and animals. This path probably marked the southeastern end of "Warriors Path," which extended from Cave Gap in a northern direction to the Ohio River. Indians traveled this well-used path en route to either a hunt or a war campaign. Prehistoric mammoth, attracted to the salt licks, left their mark by transforming the landscape into a pitted white-caked moonscape. Canebrakes, Kentucky's native bamboo, suffocated the landscape with a thicket of overgrown shrubs with undergrowth of fern.

By April 13, the group arrived at Cave Gap. Walker found a well-beaten path at the foot of the mountain where some of the trees were inscribed with Indian war marks to scare off unwanted intruders. Walker renamed the pass Cumberland Gap, after the Duke of Cumberland. Walker was partial to the British nobleman, the younger son of King George II, possibly in part to the Duke's role as a sponsor for many colonial explorations or his 1746 victory over Jacobists at the Battle of Culloden Moor.

After crossing the Gap, a place destined to see the passage of thousands of American pioneers, the party followed the path along Yellow Creek leading them down an old ford of the Shawnee River. The north side of the Gap was very steep and rocky, but the party discovered coal deposits. They left the Shawnee River near present day Flat Lick, turning northeast where they crossed some tributaries of the Kentucky River. This route forced Walker's party to traverse rugged mountains and nearly impenetrable laurel thickets. By mid-April, Walker and his men had journeyed along the western-most part of their exploration.

Pelted by rain, the group was further hampered by a bear attack that severely wounded Ambrose Powell. Along the way, Walker noted that the path's sandstone boulders softened into lowlands etched by creeks, small game, and ample timber. By April 23, the exhausted group reached a point where Clear (Clover) Creek's mouth empties into the Shawnee River. Horses famished, men weary, and supplies waterlogged, Walker decided to build a cabin four miles south of present-day Barbourville so everyone could recover from the journey.

Three of the men, however, were not quite ready to stop pressing forward. Powell and Chew accompanied Walker on a brief exploration of the north side of the Shawnee Mountains. After 5 more days and 35 miles of scouting, they had discovered ancient Indian dwellings and majestic ridge tops that offered glimpses of Jack-in-the-pulpit and the pink buds of mountain ivy nestled among towering cedars, hickories, and red oak. At one point, Walker climbed a tree and saw nothing but more severe terrain ahead. Such rugged topography led Walker to conclude that the entire region lacked fertile farmland. Ironically, if the Walker expedition had traveled another two days, they would have reached Kentucky's fertile Bluegrass region. But, having decided not to investigate the area, Walker and his companions returned to camp six days later to find that Tomlinson, Lawless, and Hughs had built a cabin, cleared some land, and planted corn and peach stones.

The final leg of the excursion began on May 11 and found the party wandering on and off of the Warrior's Path. Unable to cross the swelling Kentucky River, the men spent two days carving a canoe from a sycamore tree. While the canoe sped their progress, downed trees and constant rain dogged the party throughout the two hundred mile trek between the Big Sandy, Louisa, and New Rivers. The party attempted to cross swollen rivers, but late spring thunderstorms hampered their efforts at times. Sudden downpours often washed makeshift tents and equipment away. Frequent run-ins with wolves or elk frightened the horses and dogs, further impeding their travel. On June 5, the rains dissipated to a point that the men could ford a creek around the Louisa and Tug Forks of the Big Sandy River, an area frequented by a multitude of turkey, elk, and bear. This reprieve from bad weather allowed the party to restock their food supply. Later that month, Walker, Powell, and Tomlinson attempted to cross the confluence of the New and Greenbriar Rivers but realized the water surpassed their horse's shoulders.

On July 8, the party finally crossed the Allegheny divide and passed through the virgin coal region of western Virginia (now West Virginia) before making its way back to the Shenandoah Valley. Three days later, the group reached the Augusta Courthouse in Staunton, Virginia. By the time Walker crossed the Shenandoah Valley and passed over the Blue Ridge Mountains, he had completed the expedition in four months and seven days. While the land may have been unsuitable for farming, Walker reported that the region boasted plenty of wildlife. Walker noted in his journal that the party killed 13 buffaloes, 8 elk, 53 bears, 20 deer, 4 wild geese, at least 150 turkeys, and various small game. They could have killed three times as much meat if they wanted to.

The 1750 Walker expedition was not the first party to explore Kentucky but was the first to document its daily activities for future westward explorers. Walker's mission to secure land for the Loyal Land Company proved unsuccessful since part of the Virginia Council's provision for the expedition required settlement of the land within four years, and none of the land Walker documented conformed to the expectations for Loyal Land settlement. However, the party was successful in documenting geographical areas previously unknown, which would aid in establishing boundaries in future surveying endeavors.

Maps and names changed because of this expedition. Walker renamed the Shawnee River the Cumberland River. He also traveled through the portion of the Pine Mountain Gap known as "The Narrows" to the Cumberland Ford. Pine Gap was mapped by an eighteenth-century French explorer. Pine Gap, Cumberland Ford, and Cumberland Gap marked a triple gateway for future pioneers. The group also forged a path through Kentucky's eastern Rockcastle region, which would become a leg of the Wilderness Trail to the Bluegrass region, and they even discovered sizeable coal deposits in the Flat Top region in West Virginia. Finally, Walker's name was set in Kentucky history when he surveyed the southern boundary between Kentucky, Tennessee, and North Carolina in 1779-1780.

During a 1770 expedition, Isaac Shelby, the first governor of Kentucky, accompanied Walker on a journey that took them within a mile or two of Cumberland Mountain, at which point Walker remarked he had been there twenty years earlier. "Yonder the beech tree contains the record it," noted Walker to Shelby. "Ambrose marked his name and year upon it, and you will find it there now." Shelby examined the tree and found large legible signature: A. Powell-1750.

In June, 1931, almost 200 years later, state dignitaries, American Legion, and Foreign War veterans assembled in Barbourville to dedicate the Dr. Thomas Walker State Park, in honor of the first Englishman to have entered the state from the southeast. Crude chimney stones marked the spot of the first house built in Kentucky. The replica of the original cabin, which measured twelve feet by eight feet, stood nearby with the Cumberland River meandering in the background. Though crumbling bricks were the last vestiges of Dr. Thomas Walker's 1750 expedition into the Trans Allegheny region, the group that had gathered paid tribute to the man who had made his mark in Kentucky thirty years before Daniel Boone arrived.

BATTLE OF BOONESBOROUGH

- 1778 -

Boonesborough

MIDMORNING ON SEPTEMBER 7, 1778, DANIEL BOONE and his scouts watched four hundred Shawnees coming down the north side of the Kentucky River. The Shawnees were not alone: along with them came the British-backed French Canadian lieutenant Antoine de Quindre and his company of Detroit militia, as well as an assemblage of Wyandots, Cherokees, Miamis, Delawares, and Mingoes. The Shawnees were led by Chief Black Fish, and as they drew near to Boone and his men, Black Fish's interpreter, Pompey, summoned Boone to give him de Quindre's terms for surrender, telling Boone to take the terms back to Fort Boonesborough for consideration. Pompey also displayed a wampum belt whose rows of colored beads represented the terms for this meeting. Red beads represented the settlers' rejection of surrender; white symbolized peace for the settlers if they would return to Detroit; and black symbolized a warning against temporary reconciliation between the settlers and the Indians. Black Fish was an emissary for the British General Henry Hamilton, who wanted to thwart further settlement in Kentucky. Boone explained it would be difficult to transport a large number of women and children back to Detroit, hoping to delay any decision to discuss these terms with the fort's leadership.

The French and Native Americans let Boone and his scouts go, and as soon as Boone reached the fort, he and the fort commanders quickly assessed its defenses. They anticipated the arrival of Virginia militia reinforcements soon, but even if the Virginians arrived in time, the site for Fort Boonesborough was militarily unfavorable. The fort was close enough to the Kentucky River that the men thought they could catch all the fish they would need to outlast any battle, but the compound was vulnerable to attack on two sides. It could be attacked from a river bluff above as well as a precipitous hill to the southwest of the Lower Blue Lick. There were only sixty men and a handful of women and children in residence at Boonesborough, but guns were given to almost everyone. In an effort to mislead the attackers into believing a large garrison protected the fort, the women dressed in hunting attire and, armed with rifles, marched back and forth in front of Boonesborough's open gate. The enemy may have believed the ploy, but all hopes for ending a siege quickly passed for the settlers. They needed to prepare for a battle against an enemy who outnumbered them more than two to one.

Daniel Boone, who had been commissioned to build a road into the region and establish Kentucky's second settlement, had established Fort Boonesborough on the banks of the Kentucky River in April 1775. He had been commissioned by Colonel Richard Henderson of the Transylvania Land Company, whose interest included obtaining western land settlements to start a fourteenth colony with Boonesborough as its capital. Henderson hired explorers, such as

Boone, to scout the territory and establish civil relationships with the Indian tribes. Boone had built a solid reputation negotiating with the Cherokees as a company agent so his profile stimulated sales for the company's venture. On March 17, 1775, Henderson signed the Treaty of Sycamore Shoals with the Cherokees, offering £2,000 Sterling and trading goods valued at £8,000 while securing 20 million acres between the Ohio, Kentucky, and Cumberland Rivers for the Transylvania Land Company. No sooner had the treaty terms been signed when Boone and his party set out to mark a road and erect Fort Boonesborough.

The treaty's "sale" of Kentucky to Colonel Henderson was merely a quitclaim that resurfaced during the negotiations between Boone and Black Fish. Many Indian tribes laid claim to this triangular area between the Ohio, Kentucky, and Cumberland Rivers. The Cherokees had populated parts of eastern Tennessee and Kentucky since the 1540s but the Shawnees were beginning to populate the area seeking refuge from the heavily armed Iroquois who were driving them out of their hunting lands in Ohio and further north. The land sold to Henderson was actually land possessed by the Uges or Chickamaugans, which Boone was quick to point out to Blackfish.

Henderson hoped Boonesborough would be the capital of the newest American colony, but his plans were foiled by the events of the American Revolution. The British attempted to thwart settlers moving west by sealing its borders around Virginia in 1776. The Virginia legislature nullified the Transylvania Company's land claims stemming from the Treaty of Sycamore Shoals and made the land a county of Virginia. Colonists' westward expansion into the Ohio Valley provoked an increasingly tense British and French imperial competition. Weary settlers aggravated by British imperial policies and the taxes to support it wanted sovereignty over the western land occupied by Indians.

The Indians also sought refuge from both French and British forces who had driven them away from their territorial homelands. At the outbreak of the American Revolution, a minority of Indians who were already subjects under the British crown after the French and Indian War Treaty of Paris 1763 sided with the American rebels. Other tribes sided with the British or remained neutral, hoping to position themselves more politically favorable should the British prevail after the American Revolution.

Unbeknownst to Boone, British General Henry Hamilton, fortified in Detroit, stepped up his campaign to crush colonial settlements, especially in Kentucky. England still laid claim to land south of the Ohio River under the 1763 French and Indian War Treaty. The British commander, knowing the settlers did not have money to pay off the Indians, allied with Indians (anxious to rid their fertile hunting grounds of settlers) by supplying them with ample armaments, food, and supplies. Hamilton's campaign proved so successful that only three permanent settlements remained in Kentucky: Boonesborough, Harrodsburg, and Logan's Fort. By September 1778, Hamilton's attention had turned to Boonesborough, and he had dispatched his French Canadian allies and the Shawnee, with Black Fish as their leader, to capture or destroy the fort.

In early February, before Hamilton's attack on the fort could be arranged, Boone and thirty men went to a nearby salt lick where they were ambushed by Shawnees led by Chief Black Fish. Forced into captivity, Boone and his party observed the Shawnee culture, were given Indian names, and most importantly, obtained information that the Shawnees were going to attack Fort Boonesborough. During his five-month captivity, Boone ironically gained the trust of Black Fish and eventually became Black Fish's adopted son. During a rare solo-hunting trip, Boone ran away on horseback with a small supply of armaments.

Boone made it back to Fort Boonesborough on June 16, 1778, where he was greeted with great skepticism, especially from Colonel Richard Callaway and Major William Bailey Smith. First, the fort commanders admonished Boone for taking thirty men away from the fort and making the fort vulnerable to defense. Then, Boone had to defend his character. A few members of Boone's salt-boiling party had escaped Shawnee captivity before Boone had and had circulated a story that Boone had attempted to surrender Boonesborough and accept safe conveyance of its settlers to Detroit. In truth, Boone had used this tactic as a shrewd strategy to turn British attention away from the ill-equipped Boonesborough. Even though the accusations against him were not accurate, Boone had little time to defend himself from rumors of treason. He focused on preparing Boonesborough for battle. Amid preparations for the siege, Boone fired off a letter to the Virginia Executive Council asking for reinforcements.

As four hundred Indians and French closed in around Boonesborough's perimeter, Chief Black Fish waited one day to hear a response from the fort. When none was forthcoming, he sent word to the fort that he had a new reason for surrender: The settlers must leave Kentucky because they were trespassing on Shawnee territory. Boone and his companions refused to leave, reminding Black Fish of conditions forfeited by the Sycamore Shoals Treaty. Black Fish countered with another set of conditions: The Ohio River would act as the boundary between the two parties and could not be crossed by either side for any malicious purposes. Boone and the settlers realized there would be no more stalling and the terms of this agreement were better than the first. As both parties signed the document, the Indians seized Boone and his companions. Somehow, the men managed to break free and ran back to the fort. Due to this deception and the escape of Black Fish's would-be captives, fighting was inevitable.

On the first day of the skirmish, the Shawnees attempted to scale the fort walls but were beaten back. This tactic proved costly for the Indian warriors. Then the enemy attempted to set fire to the compound. First, they lit their blankets on fire and tried to hang the torched blankets along the palisades walls. Secondly, fire arrows, whose ends were wrapped in gun powdered-dipped rags, were shot into the compound. Luckily, several nights of rain prevented the arrows from burning through many shingles. Ingeniously Squire Boone, Daniel's brother, passed around homemade squirt guns made from old musket barrels to all the women, who thus extinguished the fire arrows.

Upon two days of an attack that produced no surrender, the Indians began to dig a tunnel to the compound wall. Watching dirt being slung into the river from an observation tower, Boone commanded the settlers to dig a tunnel that would intercept the Indian tunnel. Gunfire became so rapid during the heaviest of fighting that the slightest twitch could disclose one's position, proving fatal for both attacker and defender. Pompey, Black Fish's interpreter, brazenly popped his head near the opening of the mine to verbally taunt his enemies. Unfortunately for him, Boonesborough's best defense was its number of skilled sharpshooters, who eventually killed Pompey during one of his jests.

The siege continued for another week until the Indians made a final attempt to take the fort. Hidden in the woods, William Patton, a Boonesborough resident who had been away hunting during the siege, watched as groups of Indians repeatedly ran up to the fort walls, attempting to set it ablaze. So numerous were the fires that settlers had to climb onto the roofs to put them out, exposing themselves to volleys of gunfire. The intense barrage of fire lit up the night sky, and screams blared from within and outside the compound walls. Patton became so convinced he was witnessing the end of

Boonesborough that he quickly fled to Logan's Station to warn them of the onslaught.

However, the next morning, September 18, the settlers arose to find the enemy gone. They questioned whether this was some kind of ruse to lure them out of the fort, but eventually the settlers felt safe enough to leave the compound. They scoured the outside confines for what little remained of their crops and cattle. Men gathered up any remaining bullets littering the grounds or lodged in the fort walls to melt and recast into new ammunition. During the siege, only two settlers were killed and four were wounded. As they explored the area around the fort, the settlers counted thirty-seven bodies, but the actual number of Indian dead was difficult to figure since the Indians carried away some of their dead when retreating from the battle.

Although Boonesborough never fulfilled its destiny as the capital of America's proposed fourteenth colony, it remains historically significant as one of three colonial settlements to withstand Kentucky's tumultuous early years. Boonesborough settlers were outnumbered two to one by their enemy and still proved victorious during the longest siege in U.S. frontier history. This event fortified Daniel Boone's reputation as a skilled Indian negotiator and keen military hero.

JENNY WILEY'S INDIAN CAPTIVITY

- 1789 -

Walker's Creek

Jenny made her way along the bed of Little Mud Lick Creek, wading in its stream until the small creek joined the larger Big Paint Creek. She had been wading and walking for the past several hours, her legs heavy and her feet almost frostbitten. Exhausted, she crawled into a hollow log to get some sleep. As she lay in the log, cramped and wet, she dreamt about the Louisa River. In her dreams, she could clearly see the direction she would have to take to find the Louisa, and from there, make her way to freedom. However, her dreams didn't show parts of the creek too deep and dangerous to cross, nor did it show the thick underbrush and mountain trails Jenny would need to cover before reaching safety.

For months, Jenny Wiley had been a captive of the Shawnee and Cherokee tribes who had massacred her family. She was forced to hunt, clean and dress animals for their meat and hides, cut and gather wood for fires without the use of an ax, plant corn during harsh winter months, and carry iron ore (recently discovered by both the French and Indians) to smelt down to make bullets. Despite the trauma and nine-month enslavement she experienced, Jenny's resolve to escape strengthened. Every day, she looked for her opportunity— one day that opportunity came.

During the second half of the eighteenth century, conflict between Indian tribes and pioneers became rampant in southwest Virginia where Jenny lived with her family. Assaults by these Indians, termed "renegade Indians" by the settlers, followed a predictable pattern: sudden attack, murder, arson, the capture of women and often children, then retreat into forest with their conquests. The region between the Ohio River and Big Sandy River featured bountiful hunting trails providing a busy thoroughfare for Shawnee, Cherokee, and other southern Indian tribes. The Indians were desperate to drive out pioneers homesteading on their hunting grounds and territorial homeland.

Virginia (Jenny) Sellards was born around 1760 in Pennsylvania, the oldest daughter of a Scotch–Irish pioneer, Hezekiah Sellards. Having been raised on the frontier, she excelled in the skills of the backwoods: woodworking, sharp shooting, and weaving. She also had a keen knowledge of the outlying trails. Her joy, however, was weaving, and she spent as much time as she could creating the fabric she later used in her home and for her clothes. After marrying Thomas Wiley in 1779, Jenny and her new husband subsequently moved to Walker's Creek, Bland County, Virginia. Walker's Creek was a newly created colony established by Captain Matthias Harman, a land speculator and fervent Indian hunter.

Matthias Harman and his hunting party had attacked a band of Indians during the fall and winter of 1787–1788 while on a hunting trip to the Big Sandy River. During the fighting Harman killed the son of the old Cherokee chief. Harman recognized the old Cherokee chief, who was known to be one of the most aggressive raiders on the Virginia settlements. A bitter hatred existed between the two men since the chief had made previous unsuccessful attempts to destroy Harman's family. In retaliation for the elder Cherokee son's death, Harman feared the Indians would seek revenge and thus returned home to Walker's Creek to warn settlers of a potential Indian attack.

Harman arrived back in Walker's Creek shortly after his encounter with the Cherokees and prepared the town to be on alert. Settlers figured it was only a matter of time before the Indians came to exact revenge. In the midst of these hostilities, Thomas Wiley set out from his home the morning of October 1, 1789, intent on taking ginseng and other marketable commodities to a trading station, leaving his seven-month pregnant wife Jenny and four children alone at home with Jenny's fifteen-year-old brother. That morning, Jenny's brother-in-law and neighbor, John Borders, urged Jenny to take her children to his house as a precaution against possible attack. Jenny agreed to go, but she needed to finish weaving a piece of cloth and prepare her animals for her absence. She was not particularly concerned about leaving promptly since she knew most Indian attacks occurred after dark.

Late that afternoon, Jenny was gathering her four children to leave her cabin when eleven Indian renegades burst into her home. Jenny could offer little resistance as the renegades tomahawked three of her children to death. Her fifteen-year-old brother tried to protect them but he too was killed and scalped. Somehow, Jenny managed to fend off the Indians when they tried to take her youngest child. Her action prompted the Shawnee chief to seize Jenny and claim her as his captive.

An argument broke out between the two Indian chiefs present, a Shawnee and the old Cherokee, through which Jenny learned the men erroneously believed they had entered the Harman home. She quickly informed them that it was not the Harman cabin, which was less than a mile away from the Wiley cabin. Nonetheless, the old Cherokee chief insisted the captives be killed in retaliation for the death of his son, yet the Shawnee chief persuaded everyone to make a rapid escape fearful of any pioneers returning. As they left, the Indians set the Wiley cabin on fire.

Knowing that the settlers would send a search party out after the missing woman and her child, the group retreated over the next twenty-four hours up Walker's Creek, across Bushy Mountain, and on to Wolf Creek, Bluestone River, and finally to Great Flat Top Mountain. Jenny tried to keep up with the frantic pace of the tireless Indians, but her fifteen-month-old child slowed her down. As a result of her slowness, the old Cherokee chief seized and killed the child by swinging the baby against a nearby tree. Indeed scouts had sighted a large party following their trail, so the group changed their course, heading west with the distraught Jenny in tow. Arriving at the engorged Tug River, the group realized the only way to escape was to cross the roiling water. After seeking temporary shelter at a large rock base on the other side of the river, the group left the following day and reached the Louisa Fork of the Big Sandy River. Feeling they had eluded capture, the Indians settled there for several days to hunt, eat, and rest.

Back in Walker's Creek, the town mourned the attack on the Wileys. When Jenny had not appeared that night at the Borders's cabin as expected, John Borders and a neighbor went to the Wiley house, only to find the bodies of the slain children amid the partially burned cabin. Late the night of the massacre, Thomas Wiley returned home, but he was intercepted by John Borders before he could approach the burnt remains of his home and family. As news of the massacre spread, a search party was summoned to look for Jenny and the missing child. Harman, who was particularly knowledgeable of the frontier trails, quickly picked up the trail of the renegades, soon finding the body of the youngest Wiley child. At one point, the flooded Louisa River was the only thing that separated the Indians from the search party. The floodwaters were too dangerous for the rescue party to continue searching, and the men unanimously agreed it was useless to follow the trail further until the floodwaters subsided. Having abandoned the pursuit, the party made their way to the mouth of John's Creek and made camp. This campsite marked the spot where Harman would soon create the first permanent settlement in eastern Kentucky—by early that winter of 1790, "Harman Station" had been built.

Although she attempted to hide her pregnancy from her captors for fear of being killed, Jenny became exhausted from the forced march. By the ninth day, the group reached the present site of the city of Portsmouth on the Ohio River. Without finding a place to cross the river, the group proceeded down to the Little Sandy River. Eventually they decided to split up: the Cherokees swam across the Little Sandy River, while the remaining Indians and Jenny made their way to the Little Sandy River to spend the winter at Little Mud Lick Creek in present-day Lawrence County. The Indians thought Jenny was seriously ill, although in reality she was experiencing premature labor. Jenny was given a small cave of her own, where one winter night she delivered a boy, whom she named Robert Bruce after the legendary Scottish patriot.

Jenny and her newborn regained their strength during the following months at Little Mud Lick Creek. Three months passed before the Shawnee chief announced that the time had come to test the baby for his future ability as a good warrior. The Indians grabbed the baby from Jenny and placed him on a crudely constructed slab of dry bark and set it adrift in the swift water of a small shoal. To the

Shawnees, the feeble cries of the baby indicated he would be unable to handle the rigors of a warrior's life. Jenny rushed into the stream to rescue the infant, but immediately the Indians followed her and killed the child before her own eyes, leaving her in a solitary depression.

After nine months in captivity, her predicament changed when one day an Indian war party brought a white prisoner back to the camp. The Indians became so excited by the ritual torture of the captive that they set their sights on burning Jenny at the stake as well. The old Cherokee chief, who was responsible for the deaths of her children, admired Jenny's courageous demeanor and spared her life. He bought her from the Shawnee chief for five hundred silver brooches. The old Cherokee chief intended to take Jenny to his town in Tennessee to teach his wives how to write and weave cloth. However, shortly before she was to depart for Tennessee, the old Cherokee chief and his companions left for a daylong hunt. Jenny was carefully tied to a tree by raw thongs that had been cut from buffalo hide. A late afternoon rain had eventually weakened the rawhide thongs, causing the leather to become loose. Amazed at this unexpected stroke of luck, Jenny frantically freed herself, seized a tomahawk and knife, and immediately left camp.

She had heard of a settlement on the Louisa Fork of the Big Sandy River and hoped that it was close enough for her to reach. She quickly set out, unsure of the direction of safety. Though she was nearly discovered in the hollow log where she sought refuge, she continued down the river in the direction of her dream. At one point the roiling river water became too dangerous to cross, so she followed several forks of the Big Sandy River during an all-day trek through wind and rain. Although heavy rains obliterated her tracks, the old Cherokee chief and search party were close on her trail when Jenny caught sight of the blockhouses of Harman's Station. Fearful that Indians might appear at any minute, Jenny called out to the Harman

Station settlers but no one responded. After some time, she recognized an old family friend, Henry Skaggs. She frantically called for assistance, identifying herself and making it clear who was pursuing her.

Skaggs knew the old Cherokee chief very well and realized time could not be wasted. There was no boat at the settlement since several men had taken the only one down river to a trading post. Skaggs set about constructing a raft, tying three mulberry tree logs together with grapevines. Placing two rifles on the raft, Skaggs made a precarious trek across the swollen stream. After maneuvering the raft back across the water, Skaggs and Jenny made it to the fort just as the Indians appeared from the forest. Safely inside the confines, Skaggs fired several shots before the Indians disappeared back into the woods.

Jenny spent several months at Harman's Station recovering from her ordeal. Once the river retreated from winter snows, Harman commanded a party to take Jenny back to Walker's Creek. She finally returned to her husband after a dangerous trek back to Virginia. In 1800, the Wileys moved to Johnson County, where they raised five children born after her Indian captivity. Jenny died in 1831 at the age of seventy-one, and her descendants still reside in the area.

CANE RIDGE REVIVAL

- 1801 -

Bourbon County

THE NEWS OF A GREAT RELIGIOUS REVIVAL had spread across the Cumberland Valley, and wagons and carriages filled with people began streaming to the Cane Ridge meetinghouse in Bourbon County in central Kentucky. Most of the members of the Cane Ridge congregation offered their homes and barns to anyone needing lodging. Some farmers even left their fields unplowed so that the horses that had traveled long distances, pulling wagonloads of faithful churchgoers, could graze on the hay. By the first night of the weekend's event, more than 140 horses, in addition to the wagonloads of people that accompanied the horses, were encamped on the grounds of the church. People gazed around the grounds in amazement, speculating what the crowd might have been like if it hadn't been wet and rainy.

Saturday, August 1, began with peaceful morning services, as Christians spiritually prepared themselves for receiving communion.

The relative quiet of the morning was short-lived, however. As the day progressed, more than 10,000 people arrived by foot and in carriages. Tents were raised and covered lecture platforms were erected on and near the meetinghouse grounds. The local church members brought food and spread it out along long tables, yet this hardly fed the multitude pouring in. Throngs of people spread out listening to preaching either inside the meetinghouse or in groups scattered among the tents throughout the clearing. Still others simply walked around enjoying fellowship and the day's festivities. Eventually, the Saturday crowd swelled to 30,000, which was one-tenth of Kentucky's population at the start of the century.

For the citizens of Cane Ridge, as well as the other Kentuckians who made the trek to the small settlement, the revival was a welcome break from the hard work of frontier life, which consisted mainly of backbreaking, monotonous labor and social isolation. But even amidst the hardships of daily life, or perhaps because of it, many pioneers retained a fervent belief in Christian salvation and reconciliation.

At the time, Presbyterianism was the largest denomination in the state, but it only remained so for a brief time. Scattered populations, poor transportation, and long distances between churches required ministers to travel among their congregations. There were thirty Presbyterian ministers in Kentucky, and they served more than sixty congregations. However, those sixty congregations were not near many of the state's isolated Presbyterians, some of whom lived in very remote areas. As Kentucky's early Christians moved farther into isolated areas on the frontier, their ability to travel to established churches became more difficult. This led to reduced church membership and an increasingly indifferent religious population. Without a physical church, settlers practiced their faith wherever and whenever they could. Traveling preachers ministered to all, regardless of their formal home church or faith allegiance.

One Presbyterian minister, a man by the name James McGready, felt strongly that people wanted the opportunity to worship together and would be willing to travel for a large celebration, even if they couldn't make it to church every Sunday. McGready's compelling oratory style appealed to frontier settlers who liked the fact that he preached to the common man. At his church in Orange, North Carolina, McGready delivered fiery sermons focusing on eternal damnation for those who failed to experience a spiritual rebirth. His sermons often shunned the rise of materialism, immorality in society, and the sins of the wealthy. Such oratory won him a number of converts and enemies alike. Repeated threats of violence to his church prompted him to head west to Kentucky.

During the summer of 1800, the year before the Cane Ridge revival, Reverend McGready began what would be the first revival meeting at his Red River Church, located in Wolfe County. News of the meeting spread far and wide, and out-of-town participants were invited to camp overnight at the site. The Red River communion service and preaching initiated the tradition of camp meetings, which quickly gained popularity. Camp meetings appealed to settlers who were eager for a break in routine tasks, and the meetings were particularly meaningful to those who craved fellowship and missed attending weekly church services.

One of the observers of the Red River revival was Barton Warren Stone. A lawyer by training, Stone began his ministry in North Carolina and Georgia, eventually becoming pastor at two congregations: Cane Ridge and Concord, Kentucky in 1798. Stone was installed pastor of the Cane Ridge Congregation after the first pastor was accused of public intoxication and removed. Moved by what he saw at the Red River Church, Stone returned to Cane Ridge and immediately began to make plans for his own camp meeting the next summer. Stone was amazed that a variety of Christian denominations could worship in one assembly. Stone publicized the camp meeting for well over a month and extended invitations to Presbyterians, the ever-growing Baptist community, and the well-organized Methodist Church. Stone's hopes for a grand revival and camp meeting were more than realized. Even he was astonished when more than 30,000 people arrived!

As the Cane Ridge meeting progressed, emotional outbursts and loud displays of exultation from Saturday's crowd were heard in all parts of the campground. Religious and racial diversity transformed the event. There were eighteen Presbyterian ministers, four Methodist ministers, and several Baptist ministers visiting from Ohio and Tennessee who preached over the course of the weekend. Perched atop tree stumps or wagon beds so that the crowds could see and hear them, their sermons could be heard simultaneously. By nightfall, hundreds of candles and torches were suspended from the trees illuminating the camp site with an incandescent glow as the preaching continued.

Preachers called upon sinners to repent, and attendees listened intently near their horse-drawn wagons praying, weeping, screaming, singing, or dancing. People were everywhere. Some listened to preaching, sang hymns, or prayed in ad hoc groups scattered throughout the clearing. Others went sightseeing from group to group. And others intermingled among friends camped amidst horses, wagons, and carriages in the nearby woods. Campfires crackled, faded, then sparked in a continuous pattern over the next several days.

The preaching triggered an array of demonstrations or "exercises." The falling exercise was most common: Hundreds of participants would emit piercing screams, fall to the ground, and appear dead. Another common response to a strong religious feeling was jerking. The jerking exercise affected the entire body: Individuals would stand in one place and jerk backward and forward in some cases to the point of hitting one's head on the floor during the motion. This exercise often moved into a form of dancing in which an individual would sashay back and forth singing and praying with a "smile of heaven on their face." Some grown men and women became so taken by such exercises of faith that they crawled on their knees, barking like dogs. One eyewitness noted men, women, and children, Christians and scoffers, educated and uneducated were equally affected by bodily agitations. Stone later noted these "exercises" of faith were the result of religion becoming so low that nothing else would have caused greater attention. Although unimpressed by the emotional outbursts, Stone believed the democratic spirit of Christian unity overshadowed any negative fanaticism. Hundreds were spiritually converted through the multiple homilies of love, harmony, and salvation for all.

The central focus of the revival—the communion service—started on Sunday. More than 1,000 communicants crowded into the meetinghouse for the service. Though it was not uncommon for children to participate in many of the other events during the weekend, many families chose the male head of the household to receive communion. Communion services were not the same then as they are in many churches now. So many people wanted to participate in the communion served that at least eight waves of people were seated at the communion tables to participate in the consumption of bread and wine throughout the day. The solemnity inside the meetinghouse did not stop the fanatic religious fervor still going on outside. Nor did it stop those looking to take advantage of the moment. Included in the crowd of 30,000 were swindlers, who sold bread soaked with whiskey or vinegar to unsuspecting believers who thought they were receiving communion.

Many participants left Monday, but others stayed, stirred by the momentum of the revival celebrations and the fellowship. In fact, new arrivals continued until Thursday, when all organized activity ended. Singing, praising, and praying continued on spontaneously.

Not only did interdenominational church membership surge during the months after the Cane Ridge Revival, but also a series of events triggered Barton Warren Stone to split from the Presbyterian Church and establish the Disciples of Christ Church (Christian Church), which is one of the first Christian denominations born on American soil and not brought by Christians from Europe. In September 1803, Stone and four other Presbyterian ministers withdrew from church affiliation and created the Springfield Presbytery, which emphasized the *Bible* as the primary authority for all matters of faith and practice. Religion, politics, and social class intermingled in the years leading up to the American Revolution. The democratic principles fueled by the American Revolution spilled over into religion.

Young Presbyterian ministers, such as Stone, began to accept the belief that it was possible for man to choose his own spiritual future, not be forced to accept a predetermined one based on class, race, or religion. The notion of brotherhood and being equal in the eyes of God took on new meaning for some of the participants in the revival, including Stone, resulting in the fact that they decided to emancipate their slaves. Some revival participants came to believe slavery not only oppressed blacks physically but also spiritually as masters kept them ignorant of Christianity. The number of free blacks in Bourbon County increased from none in 1790 to 169 by 1810, in part as a result of this growing understanding of a Christian response to oppression.

What had begun as a frontier religious camp meeting had unintended consequences, namely the birth of the New Testament Christianity in America, as well as the stirrings of conscience regarding slavery. Christianity, equality, and emancipation would begin to be linked by some Kentucky frontiersmen, all because of the Cane Ridge Revival.

THE ESTABLISHMENT OF
THE PLEASANT HILL SHAKER COLONY

- 1808 -

Shawnee Run

NEWS OF THE LARGE AND SUCCESSFUL Kentucky religious revivals spread east and encouraged missionaries of various church groups to come west. It was on New Year's Day, 1805, that Issachar Bates, John Meacham, and Benjamin Youngs set forth on a 1,200-mile trek from New Lebanon, New York, to spread the Shaker faith. They traveled through the Allegheny and Blue Ridge Mountains southwest through Virginia and then proceeded through the Cumberland Gap into Kentucky. On March 7 they stopped in Garrard County to preach "the first public testimony of the Shaker gospel in the Western Country" to Matthew Houston's congregation at the Paint Lick Meeting House. The men made brief visits in Lexington and Cane Ridge, where they were warmly introduced as friends preaching the Shaker gospel for eternal salvation. Nevertheless, a growing skepticism took hold. Local revivalists and preachers, including Barton W. Stone, were reluctant to welcome the men and were somewhat suspicious of the Shaker beliefs.

The men briefly left Kentucky to cross into Ohio to preach at Malcolm Worley's congregation at Turtle Creek, Warren County. When they returned to Kentucky, Youngs brought along converts Richard McNemar and Malcolm Worley. On August 16, the party arrived at Shawnee Run, Mercer County, Kentucky, gathering at a 140-acre farm located on the Shawnee Run Creek. Local farmers Elisha Thomas and Samuel and Henry Banta welcomed the missionaries. In fact, Thomas became the first Kentucky convert and deeded his 140 acres, known as Shawnee Run, to the Shaker community in August 1806. The property conformed to the Shaker principle of isolation. The creek was hardly a navigable waterway and thus offered relative seclusion from westward settlers passing through Harrodsburg, the nearest city six miles away.

Meacham and Youngs traveled back and forth from Shawnee Run to Ohio, continuing to win converts and enemies alike. The men left one Danville, Kentucky, congregation only to find the ears and tails of their horses cut off. However, such episodes of harassment were few. Most people simply viewed the men as curiosities after they learned of the Shaker practice of dancing. On one occasion at Samuel Banta's, 200 spectators were present; and 1,200 assembled at Elisha Thomas's farm for two meetings in May 1806. Although the group was considered somewhat odd by most, by December 3, 1806, forty-four converts signed a covenant "dissolving their former ties and connections with the world . . . united together in the bonds of union and fellowship."

It took an additional two years to gather enough converts before the Shawnee Run society received formal direction to build a new colony. By fall 1808, John Meacham and the first Shaker elders lived in two log cabins situated within the center of the newest

Shaker village, called Pleasant Hill. Over the next three years, the Shakers slowly acquired land surrounding Pleasant Hill, eventually amassing more than 3,000 acres. As a result, the Shawnee Run settlement slowly diminished as the Pleasant Hill colony developed into the fourth largest Shaker society in the world.

Pleasant Hill was situated on a large, flat, and spacious plateau, quite suitable for a growing membership that peaked at five hundred by 1830. Just as they separated themselves from the world, the Shakers also divided themselves within their village. Members were divided into autonomous classes of "families." Given its number of elder members, the most spiritually advanced family was known as the Center Family. The other families, called the East, West, North, and Northeast families, were named for their socio-economic relationship with the Center Family. The population was divided into families based on their mission and industry within the commune. For example, the East Family, comprised of mostly younger members, excelled in shop and farm labor. These families contained no blood relations since all Shakers were single people who vowed to remain celibate for the rest of their lives.

Focused as they were on being productive and avoiding the temptations of the world, Shaker ingenuity, hard work, engineering skills, and creativity brought about new inventions, which spread throughout the country. The first circular saw, metallic pen, rotary harrow, screw propeller, tongue-and-groove machine, threshing machine, pea sheller, apple parer, water-repellant cloth, and the popular broad broom were invented in Shaker workshops.

The colony also established the second plumbing system west of the Allegheny Mountains. A large capacity cistern was made to collect water at the bottom of the hill. From the cistern, a 2-inch forced pump raised a column of water 125 feet uphill to a cistern dispensing the water through 600 yards of cast-iron piping to every kitchen, washhouse, and cellar in the community. The pump could force water through pipes for up to an hour, minimizing the labor of having horses haul water from nearby Shawnee Run Creek or Kentucky River.

In addition, Shaker labor spurred the growth of Kentucky's earliest manufacturing and agricultural industries. For example, the Kentucky silk industry flourished, inspired by the Shaker sisters's woven silk handkerchiefs that were exported back East or exchanged as gifts by state representatives. Other profitable agricultural enterprises were packaging and selling garden seeds and surplus fruit crops from their extensive and productive orchards. Shaker livestock was another lucrative source of income. Durham cattle; Merino, Cotswold, and Bakewell sheep; and Berkshire hogs were highly sought after by Kentucky farmers and farmers from neighboring states. But at the core of the successful Shaker farming practices, and their prospering colonies, was the firm commitment to Shaker values and beliefs.

Formally known as The United Society of Believers in Christ's Second Appearing, the Shakers were one of the first utopian societies. The Shaker movement traced its origins back to seventeenth century France. However, because of severe religious persecution in France, many believers fled to England where one of their unique tenets—the belief in the manifestation of Christ as a female—came to light.

American Shakerism originated from a group of eighteenth-century English Quakers who dissented from mainstream Quakers due to their practice of dancing during worship, "shaking" off sins of the flesh. Englishman James Wardley and his wife Jane, splintered from the Quaker community in Manchester, England, announcing they had found the female "daughter of God," which signaled the promise of a second coming of Christ. This "daughter" was Ann Lee, who had converted to the Shaker faith in 1758. In 1770, she was jailed for statements contrary to the tenets of the Quakers: celibacy, pacifism, and a liberal approach to the Bible.

During her incarceration, Lee believed she had received a divine revelation and that she was the "mother of Christ." Lee spoke of this revelation when she was released from jail, and the resulting harassment and persecution forced Mother Lee, as she became known, and eight companions to leave England and head for the shores of New York. In 1776, the same year the Declaration of Independence was signed, the first American Shaker settlement was established near Albany, New York.

Because Shakers were pacifists, they were eyed with suspicion during the American Revolution. Their other ideas also caused the establishment to look unfavorably upon the sect. Their beliefs of an egalitarian society, pacifism, celibacy, and living withdrawn from the secular world, as well as the belief that slaveholding was wrong, certainly set Shakers well outside of the mainstream of contemporary American thought.

Shakers believed that mankind's ultimate goal centered upon equal rights and privileges in all spiritual and temporal activities. This could only be achieved by separating oneself from the secular world and living in colonies of like believers. Shaker basic covenant called for open confession of sin. They did not believe in communion or baptism.

The beliefs that set them apart the most were pacifism and celibacy. They firmly believed that lust and war went hand in hand and that sex was the catalyst for human strife, war, and inequality. Celibacy was necessary in order to surrender completely to God's will. Therefore, living apart from the secular world and living communally with the genders separated, made complete sense to the Shakers. It meant, however, that there would be no children and the sect would eventually die out.

In order to combat desire, Shaker men and women lived separate but equal lives. Separate dining tables divided uniformly dressed men and women. All residence houses had two front doors and two side doors for the sole purpose of separating men and women. Women entered the right door and right stairs, while men used the left door and left stairs. Shakers believed spiritual purity was achieved through austerity. Men and women also shared equally austere lives, believing that spiritual purity was achieved through austerity and discipline.

As egalitarians, slaveholding was also contrary to their beliefs. Although some of the community's first members were slaveholders, most eventually freed their slaves. In certain cases, slaves were freed with the condition that they leave Kentucky to avoid harassment from slave sympathizers and settle in Ohio, Illinois, or Indiana. Forty ex-slaves joined the Shakers after an intensive crusade begun by the Kentucky elders to free slaves started in 1815. In some cases, Pleasant Hill elders purchased slaves as an act of goodwill, then invited them into a family as a full member. Shaker leadership even disdained hiring slave labor, but they were at times inconsistent in this belief, as when extra manpower was required.

After the Civil War, as agriculture declined and industrialization expanded in the United States, the Shaker community was challenged to continue its utopian way of life. Pleasant Hill faced increased economic pressures brought about by the steady competition from commercial processing, the cost of hired workers, and the increased expense of bringing cattle to market. Some Shakers left the colony for employment in cities while others left to homestead free government land further west. Since there were no children to carry on Shaker traditions, the community dwindled. After several years of selling off property to support the community, the Shakers eventually sold Pleasant Hill in 1910. Two hundred years later, the remaining outbuildings are now National Historic landmarks affiliated with the non-profit corporation Shakertown at Pleasant Hill, Inc., but the Pleasant Hill Shakers are no more. In fact, only a small number of Shakers remain in the entire country.

FRONTIER ABDOMINAL SURGERY

- 1809 -

Greensburg

JANE CRAWFORD WAS MYSTIFIED. AT AGE FORTY-SIX, she hadn't expected the doctors to tell her she was pregnant with twins. Now she had waited more than nine months and still the babies hadn't appeared. By early winter 1809, her local Greene County doctors believed they should seek the expertise of Dr. Ephraim McDowell, a highly regarded doctor. Traveling to her Greensburg home, McDowell examined Mrs. Crawford's enlarged abdomen and concluded the swelling was a cystic ovarian tumor, not pregnancy. McDowell explained to Mrs. Crawford that he was unaware of a tumor of that size ever being successfully removed, since opening the abdominal cavity could result in a fatal infection. Moreover, he regretfully told her that without the surgery she would die. Dr. McDowell said the choice was hers, but if she decided to go ahead with surgery, he would need for her to travel to his Danville office more than 60 miles away.

Her choice seemed impossible to make. McDowell expected Mrs. Crawford to decline surgery given the fact that the only means of travel was by horseback over a long distance in the dead of winter. Furthermore, McDowell himself was a bit dubious about the wisdom of choosing to undergo surgery. He had never attempted to remove a tumor of that size. However, much to his amazement, an exhausted Mrs. Crawford arrived at his office two weeks later.

Jane Crawford was fortunate to be the patient of a skillful surgeon such as Ephraim McDowell. McDowell, the ninth child of Samuel and Mary McDowell, was born on November 11, 1771, in Augusta County, Virginia and had grown up two miles north of the childhood home of Jane Crawford. His family later moved to Danville to follow Samuel's aspiring political career. Determined to become a doctor, McDowell traveled back East at the age of twenty to begin a three-year medical apprenticeship with Dr. Alexander Humphreys of Staunton, Virginia. In those days, an apprenticeship with a practicing physician was the accepted path to becoming a doctor. After completion of the apprenticeship, the student was named doctor of medicine. McDowell felt honored to be able to work under Humphreys, who was a distinguished anatomist educated at the University of Edinburgh, the foremost formal medical school of the day.

McDowell's love of learning and medicine was such that he wanted to continue his studies after his apprenticeship with Humphreys. Contrary to his father's wish for him to attend the University of Pennsylvania, McDowell decided to pursue medical training at the University of Edinburgh, Humphrey's alma mater. While at Edinburgh, McDowell studied anatomy under the direction of the preeminent Scottish surgeon, John Bell. Although he did not earn a medical degree, McDowell returned to the United States in 1795, establishing a successful practice in Danville and earning a reputation as one of the most skillful surgeons and anatomists west of the Allegheny Mountains. Interestingly, McDowell did not receive his medical degree until 1823, fourteen years after his pioneering surgery.

Although abdominal surgery can be dated back to 1701, when Scottish physician Robert Houston successfully drained an abdominal cyst (but failed to remove it), McDowell was the first to successfully extract an ovarian cyst. It was believed the surgery would be fatal should infection set in. At the time of Mrs. Crawford's surgery, anesthesia and antiseptics were still more than forty years from discovery. Most doctors commonly used drugs and emetics and three kinds of physics for treatment. Popular drugs and emetics included mercury, opium, ipecac, and calomel. Plasters induced blisters to draw out poisons. Cayenne pepper and brandy were used to draw water and blood.

Prior to the surgery, McDowell instructed Crawford to rest for six days. Few preparations before surgery were made given the fact that this surgery had never been performed in the manner McDowell intended. On Christmas Day, McDowell, assisted by his nephew, James McDowell, escorted Mrs. Crawford to the medical table, marked the desired location with a pen, and made a 3-inch incision to expose the tumor. Seeing the immense size of the tumor, McDowell realized he could not fully remove it. He improvised by putting a binding around the Fallopian tube and ligament connecting the ovary to the uterus to thwart blood supply to the tumor. The tumor was then cut open and fifteen pounds of dirty, gelatinous material oozed from the tumor before the collapsed sac (weighing close to seven and one-half pounds) was extracted from the incision.

McDowell's next concern was the intestines, which had protruded outside the abdomen during surgery. He promptly soaked the intestines in warm water before returning them into the abdominal wall. In order to control hemorrhaging, he turned Mrs. Crawford on her left side to permit blood to escape and thus prevent infection. McDowell grasped the Fallopian tube and ovarian ligament where he had bound them and placed stitches around the bleeding blood vessels. Between every two stitches, an adhesive plaster was applied. He then proceeded to close the external incision, leaving the ligature that surrounded the Fallopian tube out at the lower end of the incision. This practice allowed proper drainage of blood, fluids, and pus in order to decrease the chance of abscess growth after surgery. The entire operation took a mere twenty-five minutes.

McDowell advised bed rest for twenty-five days before Mrs. Crawford make her journey home on horseback. To his astonishment, he found her up making her bed five days after surgery! After she recovered, Jane Crawford returned to her home in Greene County and lived another thirty-two years. McDowell performed eleven more ovariotomies over the years, with only one death.

It was only after his third surgery that William McDowell sent an account of the surgeries to Dr. Thomas James, professor of midwifery at the University of Pennsylvania and co-editor of the medical journal *The Eclectic Repertory and Analytical Review—Eclectic Review.* Co-editor Dr. Phillip Syng Physic, a preeminent professor of surgery in Philadelphia, initially refused to publish the account. The American medical community refused to accept that such surgery could have taken place, especially on the frontier. As news of McDowell's surgery spread across the Atlantic, critics were skeptical that this surgical accomplishment could hail from an American doctor. Dr. James Johnson, editor of the *London Medical-Chirurgical Review,* cautioned readers not to believe that such a feat could have been performed in the "backwoods of America." French surgeon Auguste Nelaton even alleged that McDowell had performed his second and third ovariotomies on Negro women not for humanitarian or medical purposes but for the sole purpose of saving the property of slaveholders.

It wasn't until 1853 that McDowell finally gained credit for his achievement. Dr. Samuel Gross, professor of surgery at the University of Louisville Medical School, published a detailed report of McDowell's pioneering techniques in abdominal surgery twenty-three years after McDowell's death. Aside from his successful abdominal surgery, McDowell paved the way for many more contemporary medical practices. He studied and analyzed specimens from surgery, becoming one of the first surgical pathologists. He also introduced the current medical practice of "informed consent" or thorough explanation of methods, risks, and dangers of surgery. From the Kentucky frontier came "modern medicine," and many Kentuckians gave thanks for Dr. Ephraim McDowell whose surgical skills and understanding of anatomy saved the lives of many.

BEAUCHAMP–SHARP TRAGEDY

- 1825 -

Frankfort

KENTUCKY'S STATE CAPITAL, FRANKFORT, WAS overwhelmed by the number of out-of-towners gathering for the opening of the state legislature on November 6, 1825. As a result, Jereboam Beauchamp, a moody and impetuous twenty-two-year-old lawyer from Simpson County, Kentucky, had difficulty finding lodging. There were no vacancies at the Mansion House or Captain Daniel Weisinger's Tavern, the best-known hostel in town. Ironically, as it would later turn out, he eventually found a room at the private home of Joel Scott, the state penitentiary warden. Beauchamp told Scott he was not feeling well and needed a place to stay overnight.

After supper, Beauchamp went outside to the barn stable to feed his horse. When he returned, Scott led Beauchamp to his bedroom and reminded him to extinguish his candle when he went to bed. Beauchamp smiled and said he planned to stay awake and read for a while. Sometime after midnight, Scott heard a "hawk and spit" coming from Beauchamp's room. Upon investigating, Scott noted the door latch open and Beauchamp gone, never to return.

Early the next morning, Eliza Sharp, the wife of a prominent Kentucky politician, heard a knock at the door. She summoned her husband, Colonel Solomon Sharp, to see who was there. Before opening the door, Sharp asked who was knocking. Beauchamp responded that he was Sharp's friend, John Covington, who had gotten lost while traveling and needed a place to stay. "Are you Colonel Sharp?" Beauchamp asked. "Yes, but I don't know you," replied Sharp. Nonetheless, Sharp opened the door, and Beauchamp retorted in a pronounced shrill voice, "Then damn you, you shall soon know me." Beauchamp fatally stabbed Sharp in the chest and fled, unaware that Mrs. Sharp had witnessed the entire brawl from the top of the stairs.

News of Sharp's murder spread, and soon thereafter Governor Joseph Desha offered a reward of $3,000 for apprehension of the murderer. In addition, personal and political friends of Colonel Sharp gathered $2,000 more. This generous reward enticed many bounty hunters to attempt to track down the murderer, whose identity by this time had successfully been narrowed down to Beauchamp. By 10:00 P.M. on the night of the murder, a search party began its 165-mile trek toward Green River country with the hopes of apprehending Beauchamp. Unaware of the reward or the quick search for the murderer, Beauchamp swiftly left Frankfort after the murder and traveled 3 miles out of town for breakfast. He spent the first night in Bloomfield at the home of a relative. The second day he rode 12 miles to Bardstown, stopping for a meal and to rest his horse. After spending the night in Bardstown, he rode another 12 miles and eventually spent the third night with his brother-in-law in Bowling Green. On the fourth day, he returned to Simpson County where his wife, Ann Cooke Beauchamp, awaited his arrival. They had planned to flee to Missouri, or even to continue farther West to some remote town where no one would look for them, but their escape plan was foiled when four law enforcement officers arrived at their home and took them into custody.

The cast of characters in this tragic story had all resided at one time along the Green River in Kentucky. A Virginian by birth, the victim, Solomon Sharp, had moved to Kentucky around 1800 and eventually became a large landowner in Warren County. Sharp was a veteran of the War of 1812 and was elected to serve as a county representative in the Kentucky legislature from 1809 to 1811. Sharp had built an extensive law practice, and he expanded his political career by serving as U.S. Congressman for four years. Sharp left Washington to return to the Kentucky legislature for the 1817–1818 session and later moved his wife and three children to Frankfort after Governor John Adair appointed him state attorney general.

The second player in the drama was Ann Cooke. Originally from Virginia, Cooke's family established prominence through their landholdings. Her father's untimely death forced Ann and her aging mother to move to Simpson County to live near her brothers. Upon her arrival in Kentucky, the former Virginian society belle was relegated to living a simple rural lifestyle, fraternizing among lower social circles than she was accustomed to in Virginia. In her memoirs, *The Letters of Ann Cooke,* Cooke wrote that in 1820 Sharp invited her to a society ball and seduced her into a one-time tryst. Later, Ann Cooke overheard rumors that Sharp intended to marry another woman. Pregnant and despondent over the news that Sharp would marry someone else, Cooke confronted Sharp, who indeed confirmed his marriage plans. Several months later, Cooke delivered a stillborn child whose death sowed the seed for her revenge.

A career politician, Sharp understood the backhanded undercurrents typical of politics. During his 1821 run for attorney general, his political opponent, John V. Waring, circulated handbills accusing Sharp of fathering Ann Cooke's illegitimate child. In his defense, Colonel Sharp produced a forged birth certificate identifying the child as a mulatto and therefore obviously not his child. Cooke's hatred of Sharp began to boil over. Not only had he left her pregnant and alone, he had further vilified her by publicly claiming that the father of the baby was a black man. To Cooke's dismay, no one, including her brothers, came to her defense.

The third character in the drama, and the future murderer, was Jereboam Beauchamp. The son of a local farmer, Beauchamp was raised in Simpson County and began his adult life working as a farmhand and schoolteacher. Bored with teaching, Beauchamp turned to law and was admitted to the bar at the age of twenty. Prior to his relationship with Ann Cooke, Beauchamp maintained a cordial professional relationship with Colonel Sharp; in fact, he represented Sharp in several lawsuits between 1822 and 1824. Regardless of his professional relationship with Sharp, the naïve up-and-coming lawyer assumed Cooke's vindication as his own after he, at the age of twenty-one, became smitten with the thirty-eight-year-old Ann Cooke. Cooke agreed to marry Beauchamp in June 1824, provided that Beauchamp help her clear her name by punishing Sharp.

By the fall of 1825, Colonel Sharp decided to resign as attorney general to campaign as the New Party candidate for the state legislature. Over the preceding six-year period, Kentucky politicians became embroiled in a bitter struggle known as the Old Court and New Court Controversy. Proponents of the public bank (Bank of Commonwealth) and debtor relief battled advocates of good-faith contract and banking practices. Sharp, a New Court proponent, was dragged into the height of the warfare. The 1825 campaign for all state offices became highly acrimonious. Particular attention focused upon the election between Sharp and John J. Crittenden, an "Old Court" candidate. Sharp narrowly won but not without Crittenden bringing up the Sharp paternity case once again. Ann Cooke may have pushed the 1821 Sharp paternity allegations to the back recesses of her mind, but the 1825 resurfacing of the Cooke-Sharp allegation re-ignited her fury. Upon hearing the resurfacing of the smear tactic, Ann Cooke Beauchamp persuaded Beauchamp to kill Sharp to clear her name.

Almost six months to the day after the assassination, Beauchamp was tried, convicted, and sentenced to death by hanging. Interestingly, no physical evidence or murder weapon was ever found or produced at the trial. Along with Joel Scott's testimony, the most damaging testimony for the defense was Eliza Sharp's identification of the murderer's sharp shrill voice. Ann Cooke was also arrested, but upon examination, she was released due to lack of evidence. Released from custody, Cooke chose to stay with her husband in his jail cell. When Beauchamp's appeal for executive clemency failed, the couple resorted to planning their suicides. On July 5, the couple attempted to overdose on laudanum, but the attempt failed, prompting jail authorities to post a guard outside the cell.

The next morning, the morning of Beauchamp's execution, Cooke asked the guard for privacy while she dressed. When he left, the couple again took laudanum and stabbed themselves with a knife Cooke had smuggled in. Doctors took Cooke to the jailer's home to try to save her life. Beauchamp, severely weakened by his own self-inflicted wounds, visited his wife's deathbed before being taken to the public gallows. While his wife lay dying, Beauchamp became the first man legally hanged in Kentucky. Two companies of the Twenty-second Regiment played the chorus of *Bonaparte's Retreat* during the hanging. Beauchamp's elderly father requested the bodies for burial. The two bodies were buried locked in each other's arms within one coffin.

News of the Kentucky tragedy hit the Washington D.C. news-stands when an article was published in the *National Journal*. Additional sordid details were made public in the Philadelphia, Baltimore, New York, Boston, Charleston, Savannah, and New Orleans newspaper dailies. The tragedy inspired characters and action for six dramas and three book-length novels plus short stories, ballads, four graduate theses, and numerous poems. *The Confession of Jereboam O. Beauchamp* and *The Letters of Ann Cooke,* both autobiographically written, inspired Lexington medical student Thomas Holle Chivers to write the first bloodthirsty drama based on the Kentucky tragedy, *Conrad and Eudora* (1834). The following year, Edgar Allen Poe attempted to write *Politan: An Unfinished Tragedy, a Political Murder,* which he never finished. Charles Fenno Hoffman's (1840) *Greyslaer: A Romance of the Mohawk* was loosely based on Cooke's "wronged woman" theme. The interest in the Beauchamp-Sharp tragedy as a literary genre extended even into the mid-1900s. While working at the Library of Congress in 1944, Katherine Anne Porter introduced Robert Penn Warren, a future Pulitzer Prize winner, to the historical documents of the Kentucky tragedy upon which he based *World Enough and Time: A Romantic Novel* (1950). Although 119 years after the event, Warren rekindled the vengeful story set against the 1820s Kentucky political stage, and the saga was heard anew.

ASIATIC CHOLERA FINDS A HERO

- 1833 -

Maysville and Louisville

CHOLERA! THE VERY WORD SPREAD TERROR AND PANIC and naturally that was the reaction in the fall of 1832 when Asiatic cholera entered the river ports of Kentucky at Maysville and Louisville. The first reported case came in October when a cook in Falls City, a section of Louisville, died, prompting the Louisville city council to appoint a board of health for the purpose of recording the number of cases and deaths. Their foresight was not misguided, for between October and November, 122 fatalities were documented. There may have been more victims, yet doctors were either too busy or too lazy to document cholera cases. Moreover, some victims may have failed to seek medical attention.

Fear and the hope of avoiding the disease prompted many northern river port residents to flee south, unknowingly carrying the bacteria along with them. Generally speaking, temperature affects how cholera spreads. Cold winters routinely killed the cholera germ, while cholera cases increase as water temperature increases. Thus it was surprising to many in Kentucky that the cholera bacteria had survived over the winter and reemerged on May 29, 1833, after winter dormancy. Rumors of the first cholera cases in Maysville, Kentucky prompted 90 percent of Maysville's population to flee the city for two weeks. Within twenty-four hours, a dozen Maysville residents succumbed to cholera. Those fleeing Maysville unsuspectingly spread the disease to towns along the Maysville-Lexington road all the way to the town of Springfield.

Immediately, the disease spread throughout Springfield, which had a population of 618, and claimed its first victim, a female slave, on June 2, 1833. In fact, the disease spread so quickly within the town that on the first day it was known to have hit the town three residents were killed. The next day, five died, and on the third day, ten died. The epidemic struck rich and poor, white and black. Springfield residents began to vacate the town, abandoning construction sites and closing businesses. The rapid spread of the disease prompted George Sansbury, a Springfield hotel owner, to hand over the keys of his hotel to Louis Sansbury, his twenty-seven-year-old slave, advising him to take care of the business while he was gone.

Not only did Louis manage the hotel during his owner's absence, he also assumed responsibility for several other local businesses whose owners had fled town. Along with a woman, cook Matilda Sims, Sansbury fed and treated cholera victims, both black and white. When someone died, Sansbury and Sims prepared the body, wrapping it in sheets and burying the dead in graves he dug beside the road to the Springfield Cemetery. Why Sansbury and Sims failed to become cholera victims themselves remains a mystery. By the end of the 1833 epidemic, more than eighty deaths were recorded in Springfield alone, which meant that the town had lost more than one-tenth of its population. It is not known whether this total includes the number of slave deaths.

Nor is it known why Louis Sansbury stayed in Springfield to do his owner's bidding during the cholera panic. He could have easily fled, taking this opportunity to find his freedom in the north. It is also not known what kind of medical care he gave to cholera victims. It is extremely doubtful that he used the accepted treatments of the time, which called for opium, the lancet, and calomel. Opium was used as a tranquilizer and reduced muscle spasms. The lancet was believed to reduce congestion of blood vessels. So popular was lancet use that in some cases doctors bled up to a quart of blood from terminal cholera victims. Calomel, a white powdery compound that contained mercury, was often administered to adults and children in doses more appropriate for a horse. Calomel was believed to break down gases accumulating in the blood in the liver. Ironically, symptoms of poisoning from mercuric compounds were similar to the symptoms of cholera: vomiting, diarrhea, and renal failure. Unfortunately, Kentucky did not have a State Board of Health until 1878 so it is impossible to know the exact number of residents who died of the actual disease or the percentage that died as a result of a prescribed treatment.

It is certain, however, that Louis Sansbury did not know that Asiatic cholera is a bacterial infection that causes severe dehydration in a matter of hours unless quickly treated. Its high fatality rate is due to its transmission through contaminated water, which can become contaminated over a very short incubation period. Doctors currently treat the disease through vaccines or, if unavailable, by restoring body fluids and minerals lost through dehydration. At Sansbury's time, however, most people believed the disease was spread through poisonous gases produced by rotting vegetables. Early nineteenth-century doctors had no knowledge of the pathology of the disease and believed treatment consisted of avoiding atmospheric gases in crowded places, mid-day sun, night air, or indigestible foods. No one realized that fecal waste from outhouses thrown in shallow trenches easily seeped into streams, rivers, and drinking public wells, further spreading the bacterial contamination.

Although smallpox, typhoid, and yellow fever outbreaks occurred sporadically, the Asiatic cholera epidemics between 1830s and 1850s took a devastating toll on the state's population. Origins of the Asiatic cholera outbreak were traced to India as early as 1826. Ship travel carried the disease to the shores of the British Isles and subsequently crossed the Atlantic Ocean to the United States. New York City reported initial cases within its immigrant slums by June 1831. It was just a matter of time before the disease traveled westward through stagecoach and riverboat travel.

Nonetheless, given all the dangers of the disease, Louis Sansbury faithfully followed his owner's instruction and, due to his care and compassion for cholera victims, he became a local hero. Consequently, when George Sansbury died in 1845, his slaves—all except Louis—were divided among his children. The town of Springfield purchased Louis's freedom given his act of civic generosity twelve years earlier. The town also established a blacksmith shop for Sansbury on the corner of Walnut and Main Streets. Sansbury was a slave during the first epidemic but was freed by the time of the second epidemic of Asiatic cholera in 1854. Once again, Sansbury stayed behind tending to the needs of the sick and dying as residents fled. According to one physician's report at the time, only fifteen people decided to remain in town after forty-one residents died.

Louis Sansbury died April 12, 1861, at the age of 54. The Springfield Cemetery memorial to cholera victims mentions only Louis Sansbury by name. The inscription reads, "Louis Sansbury was a black man who cared for and buried the victims in these approximately 106 unmarked graves." Sansbury's own gravesite is unmarked among the countless other anonymous graves of African Americans in nearby St. Rose Cemetery. Nonetheless, Louis Sansbury's heroism inspired the City of Springfield to dedicate its first annual African-American Heritage Week in his honor during the summer of 2004.

DELIA WEBSTER'S EXCURSION ON
THE UNDERGROUND RAILROAD

- 1844 -

Lexington

THE SEPTEMBER SATURDAY IN 1844 STARTED like any other: Delia Webster was preparing for her weekly sewing meeting with the Lexington Female Missionary Society. The meeting went ahead as planned, yet Webster adjourned it one hour earlier than normal to take an excursion through the countryside with Reverend Calvin Fairbanks. The trip was no secret. In fact, Webster, who had been an acquaintance of abolitionists during her formative young adult years, invited several of the ladies to come with her, but since the weather had taken a turn for the worse, they declined. Webster told her landlady that this trip would require an overnight stay since Fairbanks was traveling to neighboring counties for church business. Nonetheless, she would return by the time classes started on Monday. Webster, the principal of a private Lexington female academy, knew the excursion was not simply to view the countryside or to attend to church business for that matter. This trip had an entirely different purpose—secret and safe passage for their passengers, slaves Lewis Hayden, his wife Harriet, and his stepson, Joseph. In fact, Calvin Fairbanks was not a visiting Methodist minister but used this ruse to provide a good reason for renting a driver and carriage to travel to see "friends" further north.

Webster had met Fairbanks when both attended Oberlin College (Ohio) in 1842. Those associated with Oberlin College tended to be strongly against slavery and for some time the college had aided escaping slaves. Hayden, who was a slave born in Lexington in 1811, had been looking for assistance in escaping to Canada. Hayden's first wife, Esther, and their son were the property of Henry Clay, then Kentucky's U.S. Senator, who eventually sold Esther and their son to slave traders in the late 1830s. Hayden attempted to trace their whereabouts but was unsuccessful and mourned their disappearance for the rest of his life. When Hayden married Harriet, he was committed to leave the bondages of slavery in the hopes of avoiding a similar twist of fate.

Earlier that month, Fairbanks had crossed the Ohio River to scout out Underground Railroad stations in Ripley, Ohio, and to make plans for the Hayden family's escape. At the time, Ripley was rivaling nearby sister city, Cincinnati, for Underground Railroad activity. For the planned escape, Fairbanks rented a horse and carriage from a Mr. Parker Craig in Lexington. The quintet traveled as far as Millersburg, Kentucky, which was about 224 miles from Lexington, before one of the horses became ill. As Fairbanks and his driver discussed what to do, the owner of a local tavern, Mr. Holloway, came to see if he could help. Tensions in the carriage rose as the Hayden family sat silently inside the carriage, praying not to be discovered. The entire escape would have been thwarted had Holloway looked inside the carriage to find the Haydens, disguised by a simple veil.

Delia Webster, fatigued from the journey, remained at Holloway's hotel while Fairbanks traveled overnight to Ripley with his hidden passengers, as planned. Meanwhile, word of the Haydens' escape had already spread past Lexington, which led Fairbanks to change directions and leave the Haydens at Red Oak, a town a short distance from Ripley. From there, the Haydens were able to travel during the night via Underground Railroad stations north toward Sandusky, Ohio to elude capture. The Haydens miraculously passed toll operators, eluded slave catchers and avoided ferrymen while hiding in cargo as they were transported across the Ohio River.

After Fairbanks returned to Millersburg to retrieve Webster late Sunday evening, the pair noticed a riderless horse following their carriage. The horse kept pace with them, and when Webster and Fairbanks stopped at a tollgate en route to Lexington, the gatekeeper demanded toll for the horse as well. Naturally, they refused since it was not their horse. However, the pair suddenly realized that they were being followed since their driver recognized the horse as one belonging to Parker Craig. How the riderless horse pursued the pair was a mystery, but it caused the pair to realize that someone knew their travel route back to Lexington. By the time they reached Paris, Kentucky, Parker Craig had caught up with them and demanded an explanation as to why they had stolen his horse, which had stuck by their carriage for miles, and to demand payment for it. Fairbanks denied the accusation and refused to pay, so Craig slyly suggested the trio return to Lexington to negotiate a compromise. What Fairbanks and Webster did not know was that Parker Craig was aware of their Underground Railroad activities and had set the pair up with the ill horse in an attempt to thwart their plans to help the Haydens.

The fall horse races were going on in Lexington at that time, so the town was full of raucous ruffians, creating the perfect atmosphere for Parker's plan to expose Webster and Fairbanks as traitors and "slave stealers." Upon reaching Lexington, Craig grabbed Fairbanks and loudly accused him of "horse stealing." Immediately, a rowdy mob closed in on the two, tying up Fairbanks and arresting him. Webster hurried to her boarding house and found that her room had been ransacked and letters from Fairbanks detailing escape plans had been stolen. She too was arrested and charged with assisting in the escape of three slaves. Webster strongly disputed the charge that she was a slave stealer—she was an abolitionist. Many Kentuckians equated the two terms, but Webster contended she was not someone who went south to incite slaves to leave their owners. Rather, she helped slaves who had already decided to escape find safe travel on their way to freedom—a distinction not obvious to slave owners at the time.

This 1844 incident perplexed many Kentucky slaveholders. They could not fathom why a well-educated white Northern female would attempt to "steal" personal property. Webster's antislavery sentiments may be attributed in part to the fact that she was raised in Vermont, a state with strong anti-slavery sentiments that dated back to 1777 when it prohibited slavery in its state constitution. Moreover, Webster was strongly influenced by the antislavery rhetoric of Reverend Harvey Leavitt of the Congregational Church of Vergennes, Vermont. In addition, she had been educated at Oberlin College, an antislavery hotbed. Given all this, her views on slavery were firm and not to be changed.

After her arrest, she was imprisoned for three months without trial or any formal court procedure. Eventually, she was brought to trial where she pleaded not guilty. The majority of the jurists were slaveholders and quickly convicted Webster of violation of the Fugitive Slave Act of 1793, a federal law legalizing the recapture of fugitive slaves even if these fugitives were living in a free state. The law also prohibited American citizens from assisting slaves. Webster was sentenced to two years in the state penitentiary. However, the jury also recommended an immediate pardon. No doubt the jury was swayed by the fact that the evidence presented against her was weak. Perhaps equally important was the fact that Webster had social connections with prominent Kentuckians with strong ties in legal circles. Governor William Owsley pardoned Webster, despite many protests, on February 24, 1845. Humiliated yet strangely empowered by her incarceration, Webster left town and the Lexington Female Academy, which she had established after teaching in Georgetown, Flemingsburg, and Cynthiana, and returned to teaching in New York. At the same time she busily raised money from her abolitionist friends.

Webster returned to Kentucky in 1854 with the necessary financial backing to purchase a 600-acre farm in Trimble County, known as Mount Orison, with the intention of establishing a farm and school. Farmed by free blacks, the farm actually operated as an Underground Railroad station for slaves seeking freedom. Neighboring landowners and slaveholders were not happy having free blacks nearby and used intimidation and physical harassment to chase twenty families off Webster's property. In the spring of 1854, several free blacks mysteriously disappeared from the farm. Recognizing danger, Webster fled to Madison, Indiana, to avoid arrest should her Underground Railroad activities become exposed. During her absence, the property was ransacked and local slave owners took steps to keep the farm from operating. Three years later, slaveholders blocked Webster's attempt to secure a credit extension on the farm. Webster circumvented this tactic by gathering financial support from several Boston financiers who established the Webster Kentucky Farm Association to save her Mount Orison. This financial rescue paved the way for Webster to plan building an integrated school for the poor, which further outraged her neighbors.

Even the end of the Civil War did not make life easier for Webster. Emancipated slaves, leaving their former owners, no longer needed to travel the Underground Railroad. Even though Webster had no active role in the travel of these former slaves, she was still a pariah in her neighborhood. Over a thirteen-year period, arsonists destroyed seventeen houses, four barns, and eventually Webster's own home at Mount Orison. Since only $300 was covered by insurance, Webster fell further into debt, as did the Webster Association, eventually causing it to be dissolved. After Webster lost Mount Orison to creditors in 1869, she moved back to Madison. Although her fame and notoriety were gained through her Underground Railroad efforts, Webster was at heart a teacher and a social activist. In Madison she returned to education, this time teaching classes in the basement of an African American Baptist Church for children who were denied admission to schools because of their race. Always fighting for justice and equality, this intrepid woman continued actively working for civil rights. At the time of her death in 1904 at the age of eighty-seven, Delia Webster was a dedicated worker in the fight for woman's suffrage.

A GOVERNOR STRIVES
FOR NEUTRALITY

- 1861 -

Frankfort

THE FIRST SHOTS FIRED BY THE CONFEDERACY at Fort Sumter in 1861 prompted President Abraham Lincoln to contact several Northern governors requesting 70,000 men for the Union army. Kentucky Governor Beriah Magoffin quickly wired his response back to Lincoln: "Your dispatch is received. In answer I say *emphatically* that Kentucky will furnish no troops for the wicked purpose of subduing her Sister Southern States." News of Magoffin's refusal elated the Confederate Secretary of War, L. P. Walker, who hurriedly sent Magoffin a request for troops to aid the Confederate army. Magoffin refused Walker's request as well. Beriah Magoffin not only denied militia for the Union or Confederate cause, but he also sent out identical memos to Jefferson Davis and Abraham Lincoln requesting both sides respect his state's neutrality. Northern and Southern leaders were bewildered by Magoffin's action. Each wondered whether he was secretly plotting some sort of deception.

Lincoln was particularly confused given the fact that Magoffin had been elected governor in 1859 by a majority of pro-Union Democratic voters. Nonetheless, Magoffin's views were pretty clear. He endorsed slavery and states' rights but not the division of the nation. During his first year in office, Magoffin supported the efforts of John Crittenden to arrange a compromise to appease both secession advocates and opponents. When the Crittenden Compromise failed, Magoffin turned to the states bordering Kentucky (Tennessee, Missouri, Indiana, Ohio, West Virginia, and Virginia) to form a neutral buffer zone between the North and the South. With the hopes of keeping Kentucky out of the impending war, Magoffin officially declared Kentucky's neutrality by seeking full legislative approval to this action in May 1861.

Despite this action, the Confederates believed it was only a matter of time before Kentucky seceded from the Union. So sure was the governor of Tennessee of this that he sent a representative to Frankfort to arrange defense preparations along the Ohio River. Once there, the representative was politely informed that such preparations would violate Kentucky's neutrality. Assuming conflict was imminent, Magoffin sent an agent to New Orleans to buy arms for the ill-equipped state militia. Military supplies were extremely scarce, and Magoffin had to purchase supplies where he could find them. Nonetheless, this action was construed by many as demonstrating that Magoffin was sympathetic to the Confederacy.

Both the North and the South were keenly interested in Kentucky's strategic location. The Confederacy needed access to the Louisville & Nashville Railroad to carry supplies to the South. To assure this access, the Confederate commanders stationed troops within 50 yards of the Kentucky border and constructed Forts Henry and Donelson on the Tennessee and Cumberland Rivers, just over the Tennessee state line. The Union also wanted to protect Kentucky's valuable commodities consisting of hemp, tobacco, flour, and mules. (Kentucky ranked second in mule production by 1860—a profitable component to the operation of a plantation.) The Union handled Kentucky diplomatically because the state influenced waterway traffic along the Ohio, Mississippi, Tennessee, and Cumberland Rivers. Control of all four of these rivers was critical to the success of either Union or Confederate strategies. The North established camps across the Ohio River directly opposite Louisville and Newport. Initially, both sides respected Kentucky's neutrality but this situation changed when the rebel army moved into Columbus and Bowling Green, Kentucky, in September. Union troops responded by taking Paducah. Soon after, Union troops moved into Kentucky, and state legislators passed a series of resolutions effectively ending Kentucky's neutrality.

Reluctantly, Kentucky entered the conflict, but decisions for choosing the Union side rested with the state legislators, not Magoffin. Given Magoffin's refusal to send troops to the Union army, Kentucky's Unionists distrusted him. After they gained a two-thirds majority in both houses of the General Assembly in the summer 1861, his vetoes were routinely overridden. Moreover, legislators lacked any confidence that Magoffin could function objectively as commander in chief of the state militia. A "military board" was created to help oversee the militia, but clashes between Magoffin and the board rendered the state militia useless.

The Kentucky militia could not prevent an army from entering the state. Knowing this, in early July 1862 Confederate General John Hunt Morgan began extensive raids fortifying his renegades within a stone's throw of Frankfort without even a challenge from the state militia. Morgan trekked more than 1,000 miles in a 3-week period capturing 17 Kentucky towns, destroying supplies, and recruiting more than 300 men as he eventually retreated back south. Another blow to the state's militia occurred when Union military officers, after their arrival in the state, instituted martial law, thereby removing civil authorities and judges who were believed to have pro-Confederacy leanings.

Dismayed that his constitutional powers were being thwarted by the Unionists as well as the pro-Southern contingency, Magoffin called a special session in August 1862. In his speech he tried to explain the inaction of the state militia as well as the military board's violation of Constitutional and civil liberties. He declared that the purpose of the war had shifted from Union preservation to the emancipation of slaves (an institution Magoffin personally upheld). This direction differed from Kentucky's initial understanding that the Union would be preserved. Halfway through his speech, Magoffin switched his rhetoric, with the hope of swaying legislators to believe in his leadership abilities. He claimed he was the victim of character assassination by the very individuals who had formally approved Kentucky's neutrality just a year earlier. He concluded the speech by hinting that, if necessary, he would honorably resign for the sake of Kentucky.

His address failed completely. Magoffin could not win over his enemies with his pronouncement that he was innocent of treason anymore than he could convince them that the legislators' course of neutrality was correct. Magoffin attempted to reiterate that he was acting on behalf of their interests to maintain the union. The Whig press continued to write negative editorials about him with the same intensity since his inauguration. The *Louisville Daily Journal* and the *Frankfort Commonwealth* stepped up attacks on Magoffin's loyalty as well. Unable to govern under these circumstances and deluged with bad press, Magoffin resigned but with the condition that he choose his successor. He chose former Speaker of the House James F. Robinson. In a final act of hypocrisy, the legislature passed a resolution thanking Magoffin for his services and complimenting his willingness to sacrifice for the sake of a unified Kentucky. Magoffin had learned that in politics and in war, it is impossible to please the opposing factions.

During a five-month period (May–September 1861), Kentucky adopted an official policy of neutrality. However, this policy could never be fulfilled, given that Kentucky could hardly prevent both Unionist and Confederates from infiltrating the state. Furthermore, its railroad routes were a valuable transportation source for both federal and rebel forces. The state truly endured its own division during the Civil War. Of the war's prominent military leaders, sixty-seven natives/residents of Kentucky became Union generals and thirty-eight became Confederate generals. To this day, the question of whether Kentucky was a Confederate or Union state remains. Approximately 103,000 Kentuckians served both the Union state militia and the Union Army while 35,000 to 40,000 Kentuckians served as volunteers for the Confederate Army.

CIVIL WAR REFUGEES' EXPULSION
FROM CAMP NELSON

- 1864 -

Nicholasville

REFUGEES AND REFUGEE CAMPS ARE ALWAYS A result of war. Men, women, children, even soldiers become refugees, and conditions for them are rarely good. For the black slaves at Camp Nelson (located south of Nicholasville in Jessamine County) at the end of the Civil War, not only were conditions harsh and bleak, many were expelled from the camp itself, set upon by bands of white thugs, or denied basic necessities. Some suffered all of these indignities. The Burnside family was just one of many to experience such depravity.

John Burnside, a former slave and Union soldier from Garrard County, told of his family's expulsion from Camp Nelson on November 28, 1864, in his sworn affidavit for government officials. Prior to their arrival at camp, his wife and children had been threatened by their owner, William Royster, who falsely accused them of informing federal authorities about Royster's fugitive rebel son. Fearful for their lives and needing protection, Burnside's sister appealed to one of Camp Nelson officers for help. Colonel Sedgwick agreed to take the family into the camp for protection. Unlike white soldiers, the families of black soldiers did not receive any federal aid; consequently, Mrs. Burnside worked as a cook or washerwoman. Two months later, the Provost Guard abruptly ordered the Burnside family out of the camp. Allowed to leave with only the clothes on their backs, a military wagon unloaded the family deep into a forest 7 miles from camp. Unsheltered in the woods, the family was exposed to rain, gusting winds, and freezing temperatures.

The Burnside family was hardly alone. More than 400 slave refugees, mostly women and children, were forced out of Camp Nelson by armed Union soldiers that month. Undernourished and poorly clothed, 250 refugees returned to Camp Nelson after the order was reversed several weeks later, but 102 refugees died shortly thereafter. This was not the first time commanding officers drove off refugee families. It was the camp's eighth expulsion. What precipitated this expulsion was the camp's need to build up supplies and troops in preparation for its last military assault into Virginia. Aside from the fact that refugees were occupying necessary space, the women and children of black soldiers in Kentucky were not free. Because they were slaves in a non-seceding state, Kentucky slaves were not freed by Lincoln's January 1, 1863, Emancipation Proclamation, which only freed slaves in the South. Living at Camp Nelson illegally, slave refugees dreaded the thought of returning to slavery.

Camp Nelson was of strategic importance for the Union army because it served as a launching point for an invasion into Confederate-held eastern Tennessee. Located at the mouth of the Hickman Creek, Camp Nelson was protected by the high cliffs and bluffs of the Kentucky River. Its location close to the Cumberland Gap fortified its position as a supply depot for Union troops. Although initially intended to be a recruiting station for white soldiers, Camp Nelson eventually became the largest recruiting and training center for African American soldiers, designated United States Colored Troops (USCT).

Recruitment of Kentucky slaves, both free and those desiring to serve in the military began in the western portion of the state. By August 1863, thousands of drafted slaves descended into Camp Nelson to begin building roads, bridges, and rail lines, much to the chagrin of slave owners. Slaveholders received $300 compensation per slave in return for their services performed in the military. Enlisted free blacks and slaves were immediately sent to military camps outside the Commonwealth in order to thwart any possibility of slaveholders attempting to kidnap their former slaves. In June 1864, all draft restrictions were lifted, and by this time, any black male could enlist in the Union army, with or without his owner's consent. This announcement prompted a drastic surge of black enlistees at Camp Nelson. Black enlistee enrollment more than doubled in one month: 574 black men enlisted in June while 1,370 enlisted in July.

In one year alone, 40 percent of the eligible black men in Kentucky joined the Union army. As a consequence, their families followed them to Camp Nelson. Many of the women and children fled slaveholders who were furious that the federal government had drafted their slaves and thus taken their legal property without their consent. In retaliation, these slaveholders treated the families that were left behind cruelly. Some of the black soldiers' families were tortured and killed, while others were expelled from their slaveholder's property since they were now nothing more than a financial burden since their labor-producing male relatives were gone. With no other place to go, slave families followed their husbands and fathers to Camp Nelson in the hopes of finding a safe haven from slavery.

Their dreams were quickly dashed upon arrival at Camp Nelson. Refugees were denied simple rations such as firewood, food, clothing, shelter, and basic health care. Communicable diseases spread quickly due to the crowded living conditions. There were so many cases of smallpox, measles, and other illnesses that the medical staff could no longer handle the situation. Soldiers closed makeshift schools for the refugees, turning the emptied buildings into barracks. Even though the military tried to get rid of the refugees, they quickly returned. Camp Nelson's commanding officers instituted a series of standing orders in the late summer of 1864 to expel all black women and children unfit for service (such as cleaning, cooking, or laundry) and to send them back to their owners. The situation reached a climax in November 1864 when post commander General Speed Fry took action not only to expel the refugees from the camp, but also to burn their cabins to keep them from returning.

This incident gained national press and, thanks in part to intervention by an abolitionist minister, John G. Fee, the standing order was reversed, and Fry was relieved of command. Fee had arrived at Camp Nelson as a volunteer missionary, quickly establishing schools and a church as well as administering an official refugee home. Newly installed post commander Captain Theron Hall, along with Fee, opened the government-sponsored Refugee Home to offer some assistance to the swelling refugee population. By the time the Refugee Home opened in January 1865, Camp Nelson spread out over 4,000 acres and was functioning at capacity. Two months later, women and children who had male relatives serving as soldiers at Camp Nelson were legally entitled to sanctuary through the 1865 Congressional Act. As a result, thousands took advantage of this twist of events and descended upon Camp Nelson.

Feeding, clothing, and managing the heavily populated camp was difficult. Hall hastily constructed 29 buildings to accommodate the more than 3,000 refugees who entered Camp Nelson. Each building housed 100 to 150 people. Problems with sanitation and infectious disease escalated, as did the level of noise. The high mortality rate of refugees rivaled the pace of construction. More than half of the 600 women and children in refugee quarters suffered from pneumonia and smallpox, and most died.

The end of the war in April 1865 swiftly curtailed construction. In fact, the federal government initiated action to dismantle Camp Nelson. However, this did not stop a new flood of refugees from flocking to Camp Nelson. Although all slaves became free at the end of the Civil War former slaves had no place to live. Once again, federal officials attempted to force refugees out, but with little success. There were still more than 2,400 women and children within the camp's perimeters in September 1865, a month after the war ended. Outgoing military personnel turned the camp over to missionaries to educate and provide medical assistance to the refugees. Staff and management problems were pervasive. The line of demarcation by which workers fell became confusing given the camp was managed by the Union army but regulated by the American Missionary Association, the Freedman's Bureau, and the Sanitary Commission. Furthermore, the missionaries and other volunteers could not contain the gangs of armed thugs or "regulators" (disguised as federal agents) who attempted to breakup the predominantly black community.

Bands of white regulators moved through camp, breaking into makeshift tents and cottages to steal what little the refugees had. In November 1866, thirty white regulators swept through Camp Nelson, forcing many blacks to flee into the night. However, former slave and Union soldier John Burnside refused to flee his home. He fought his attackers and mortally wounded one. The mob eventually stormed his home and beat him mercilessly, leaving him for dead. White renegades continued harassing the now-free blacks who remained in the area for years after the war ended. Nonetheless, Camp Nelson still had a role to play in the lives of former slaves—it became the chief center in Kentucky to issue emancipation papers to former slaves. All told, between 9,000 and 10,000 black soldiers passed through its entryway during the course of the Civil War.

THE CREATION OF THE
LOUISVILLE SLUGGER

- 1884 -

Louisville

SEVENTEEN-YEAR-OLD JOHN A. "BUD" HILLERICH HAD been working at his father's woodworking business all day when he decided he deserved a break. It was a warm spring afternoon in 1884, and Bud decided there was no better way to spend the rest of the day than down at the ball diamond, watching the local team, called the Louisville Eclipse. The team's star outfielder was Pete "The Gladiator" Browning. During the course of the game, Browning broke his bat, which is never good but is especially bad for a superstitious player in the midst of a hitting slump, as Browning was. After the game, Bud approached Pete and offered to make him a new bat. Pete accompanied Bud to his father's woodworking shop, where Bud began to hand-turn a new bat according to Browning's specification. The next day, "The Gladiator" stepped up to the plate and belted out three hits with his new Bud Hillerich bat, dubbed the Falls City Slugger. So impressed were Pete's teammates that when they found out where he got the bat, they requested a batch of Hillerich bats as well.

Thus was born the Louisville Slugger, a type of baseball bat that was custom-made for baseball players. Until 1884, baseball players across the country had their local woodworkers make their bats, but the Hillerich family revolutionized bat making by customizing each bat to a player's specifications. Initially the company manufactured wooden bats for amateur players, but the Louisville Slugger's reputation won admirers within the major leagues. Players could select the type of bat by weight, length, style and selection of wood. Furthermore, amateur players could purchase the Slugger model of their favorite professional player.

The story of Bud and "The Gladiator" describes the making of a legendary baseball bat, but it isn't the only story of the genesis of the Louisville Slugger. In a 1914 *Louisville Herald Magazine* interview, Bud Hillerich reported that Pete Browning approached Bud to design a new bat during a hitting slump. Browning, his old bat in hand, reportedly told J. F. Hillerich, "I can't hit a thing with it." Hillerich replied, "Well, bring it back, and I'll put a home run in it for you." Bud Hillerich set the old bat in a lathe and scratched a circle around it. Later that day, Browning hit a home run and, ever after, Louisville sluggers were made with rings around them.

Interestingly, in J. F. Hillerich's, Bud's father, 1929 obituary in the *Louisville Times,* another version of this same tale recounts that it was John F. Hillerich, himself, who was the famous bat builder.

Unfortunately, there is no conclusive evidence to verify the authenticity of either of these two stories. In fact, a third story is also told, which attributes the birth of the Louisville Slugger to both Bud and J. F. Hillerich, but has nothing to do with Pete Browning.

Teenage Bud was an amateur baseball player whose custom-made bat had been lost or stolen while Bud was a member of Louisville's Morning Star team in 1883. Recovered during the 1884 season, the bat fell into the hands of pitcher Gus Weyhing, who was at that time still a minor league player on the cusp of breaking into the major leagues. (Once a major leaguer, Weyhing would go on to win 264 games for nine major league teams over the course of his career.) Weyhing passed Bud's bat along to several players on his team, was impressed by the quality of the Hillerich bat, and requested that J. F. Hillerich make more. J. F. agreed to make more bats, if in exchange the players never asked him to make the bats again. The current generation of Hillerichs believes the first Louisville Slugger was most likely hand-turned for Bud, if not by him, lending this version of the bat's origin more credence than the others.

However, this is not the end of the mystery. Arlie Latham noted in a 1937 *Baseball* article that he, in fact, was the first recipient of the Louisville Slugger. Latham, nicknamed "the Freshest Man on Earth," taunted opponents and fans alike as third baseman and lead-off hitter for the St. Louis Browns. According to him, Latham visited the Hillerich woodworking shop after he broke his bat during a game in either 1883 or 1884. J. F. Hillerich agreed to hand turn a bat for him to use for the next day's game. This account was verified by a 1942 letter from Bud Hillerich, but baseball historians debate its reliability, believing the letter is more likely a public relations stunt. It seems unrealistic Hillerich would have custom-made a bat for a hitter with a mediocre career average (.269). J. F. Hillerich initially did not want his business to have anything to do with baseball, so most likely if he were to have agreed to make a bat, it would have been for a player he strongly admired. This wouldn't have described Latham, who had earned a reputation around town based on his clubhouse vulgarity and exaggeration more than his hitting prowess.

Although the tales of its origin differ, each story indicates that Bud and J. F. Hillerich were actively involved with the making of the first Louisville Slugger bat. J. F. Hillerich, a German immigrant, opened his Louisville shop in 1859, manufacturing bedposts, rolling pins, stairway posts, and balusters. The only thing J. F. Hillerich & Sons produced in the sporting goods line was an occasional bowling ball and pins. In fact, the elder J. F. Hillerich had no desire to pursue bat manufacturing since he was making a successful living producing the newly patented swing butter churn. Furthermore, J. F. Hillerich knew America's up-and-coming pastime was scandal ridden during its infancy, and he had no desire to participate in something he thought was somewhat tainted. In fact, the Louisville Grays, another of Louisville's early teams, which had made a promising entry in the National League, had to drop out of the league in 1877 after four players fixed a game.

As baseball grew in popularity after the Civil War, professional leagues instituted some equipment restrictions. In 1859, the Professional National Association of Baseball Players governing committee instituted a restriction that forbid any bat larger than 2½ inches in diameter. Ten years later, a rule designating bat length was adopted, limiting the length to a maximum of 42 inches. By 1887, Hillerich & Sons tested several varieties of wood, finally settling on Northern white ash, grown in Pennsylvania and New York. White ash was favored for its strength, resiliency, and weight—three characteristics that combined to give batters greater power and drive.

J. F. Hillerich may have entered into bat-making reluctantly, but Bud quickly saw its potential. Disappointed that his own baseball career had been sidelined after a shoulder injury in the late 1880s, Bud not only began manufacturing hand-turned bats for up-and-coming players, he invented a centering device for a lathe and an automatic sander. The success of the Hillerich bat was due in part to the company's willingness to customize each bat for different players' specifications. Lou Gehrig used a Slugger bat, Model GE69, with a 2½–2⅝ barrel, 34-inch length, and weighing 38 ounces. Babe Ruth and Hank Aaron used similar Slugger 300Pro Model bats, although Ruth's bat weighed 42 ounces and Aaron's weighed 33 ounces.

Initially, Hillerich bats were known as the Falls City Slugger, so named because Louisville sat across from the Falls of the Ohio River. Who chose the Louisville Slugger name remains another mystery, but it is believed league players created the nickname. However, the success of Pete Browning, one of Louisville's very own, was no less of a reason to honor this American trademark. One of the American Association's best infielders, Browning's standout rookie season included a hitting average of .510 and on-base percentage of .430. Browning was the AA's batting champ in 1882 with a career average of .343 eventually hitting .402 by 1887. The timing of the growing popularity of the Louisville Slugger coincided with the city rebounding from baseball scorn and reentering the American Association. In 1894, the Falls City Slugger was officially trademarked as the Louisville Slugger in the U.S. Patent Office. Browning would not be the last of baseball's rising stars to grip the Louisville Slugger: He was joined by Hugh Duffy, Eddie Collins, Ty Cobb, Ted Williams, Jackie Robinson, Pete Rose, and Derek Jeter, among many others.

LOUISVILLE TORNADO AND
FOUNDING OF THE SOUTH'S FIRST
FREE CHILDREN'S HOSPITAL

- 1890 -

Louisville

ON MARCH 27, 1890, THE CITIZENS OF THE southwest corner of Louisville prepared themselves for an evening thunderstorm and a possible tornado. This wasn't out of the ordinary—Kentucky springtime's are prone to fluctuations between mild temperatures and severe weather. Little did they suspect, however, that the approaching front would actually spawn several tornadoes. Earlier in the day, the weather was typical for early spring—fair with little chance of rain. By late afternoon, however, a telegraph from Washington's National Weather Service signaled Louisville that it sat in the path of "violent atmospheric disturbances." The barometer had fallen so quickly throughout the afternoon that a Louisville police sergeant noticed the mercury in the glass tube "trembling."

The telegraph was correct. Louisville was directly in the storm's eye. The tornado's 300-yard path of destruction started in the newly suburbanized Parkland portion of the city, demolishing thirteen homes and assorted stables, barns, and outhouses. As the twister moved northeast toward central downtown, its path was haphazard. The twister merely skimmed the rooftops above mansions dotting the south side of Broadway Street, but it flattened the Third Presbyterian Church and completely destroyed houses along 5 blocks of the north side of Broadway Street. As it moved, the tornado seemed to gather strength, saving its most destructive fury for the downtown business district.

As the tornado moved through town, two local lodges, the Odd Fellows and the Knights and Ladies of Honor, were conducting an initiation ceremony on the third floor of the Falls City Hall. On the second floor, a dance class of seventy men and women had concluded, but several people remained behind, seeking shelter while the storm passed. It soon became apparent, though, that the storm was not going to pass them by. The noise of the tornado had crowds jamming the exits, trying to get out of the building before it was leveled. In a matter of seconds, the roof was blown away and the two floors with its 250 occupants were subsequently flattened, its rubble of bricks, mortar, and strewn timber spilling onto Market Street. One survivor noted the floor buckling under his feet moments before the impact. Events happened so quickly that no one made it out of the building without having to crawl out of the wreckage. The Falls City Hall was the site of up to seventy-six fatalities.

But the tornado was not done. The twister continued to wreck havoc on downtown Louisville, destroying the Union Railroad depot, thirty-two industrial buildings, ten tobacco warehouses, five churches, and three schools before crossing the Ohio River and creating a path through Jeffersonville, Indiana. Its destruction didn't end until it finally crossed over the Ohio River back into Kentucky three miles upriver from Louisville, toppling the top 120-foot tower of the Louisville Water Works and shutting off water service to the city for a week. More than 600 buildings were damaged or destroyed, leaving an estimated $2.15 million in property damage. German and Irish immigrant and poor African American neighborhoods sustained the brunt of the damage. Rubble and debris reached 30 feet in height in various spots throughout the city, preventing rescuers from reaching victims trapped in the wreckage.

Falls City Hall rescuers heard the anguished cries of victims as they furiously attempted to move debris barehanded. Locomotive headlights were brought in to illuminate rescue efforts. The first evening, rescuers uncovered the bodies of three girls who had hidden in a closet. Half an hour later, a woman and three of her children were pulled alive from the wreckage. Her husband pleaded for help to find their five-year-old daughter, who was still trapped inside, but a fire broke out. Ignited by the timber, straw, and coal that had heated the building earlier that night, the firestorm spread quickly. Rescuers could hear the impassioned groans and screams of those trapped intensify as the fire spread. The gravity of the situation was further magnified when rescuers finally reached the burned, mangled, and severely injured adults and children, and there was no predestined place to take them. Sick or injured children were rarely hospitalized. The city lacked a hospital to meet the needs of children whose injuries and diseases were often pathologically different from adults.

Meanwhile, as the Falls City Hall rescue efforts carried on, the dean of Louisville's Hospital College of Medicine was delivering an emotional speech at the meeting for the founders of the free regional children's hospital. Seven years earlier, the city's Board of Trade had created the Charitable Organization Society to coordinate efforts to reduce poverty and to initiate child advocacy reform. One of its founders, Mary Lafon, began spearheading the Children's Free Hospital movement. Lafon had had a successful career administering a local orphanage. She had also organized Louisville's Free Kindergarten Movement and the Equal Rights Association. Lafon centered her activism on impoverished women and children who were still considered legal property of their husbands and fathers at this time. The closing of the volunteer-run Kentucky Infirmary twenty years earlier prompted Lafon to take action to initiate financial and medical backing for a free children's hospital to serve not only Louisville but also the underserved Appalachian region.

Lafon's first action was to solicit supporters. This was not easy since charities at that time were divided among religious groups as well as Union and Confederate causes. However, one of Lafon's best traits was her ability to unite differing religious and political factions. She enlisted the support of Dr. John Larrabee, founder of Louisville's first day nursery for children of working mothers, and Dr. Ap Morgan Vance, a pioneer orthopedic surgeon. She sought financial support from her banker cousin, Edmund Halsey, founder of the Columbia Finance and Trust Association. She was also successful in getting both Union and Confederate sympathizers to support the idea of the hospital. And she was successful in encouraging fourteen fellow parishioners of her local Presbyterian Church to act as the initial core for the free children's hospital. The Warren Memorial Presbyterian Group decided to schedule their first meeting on March 28—the day after the tornado.

On March 28 snow fell on the smoldering ruins as the city began to clean up and continue recovery efforts. As news of the tornado's destruction spread across the country, curious spectators began to travel to Louisville. As if curious bystanders were not enough of a problem, pickpockets and looters pillaged city streets. The state militia was called in to alleviate both problems and restore normalcy. Late that afternoon, Mary Lafon and her volunteer group assembled the Hospital Circle and officially established the first regional children's hospital. The Hospital became the first children's hospital in Louisville to admit patients without regard to race, religion, or the ability to pay. The need for such a hospital had been obvious to some, but the destruction of the previous day's tornado made the need brutally clear to all.

Despite the destruction of the 1890 tornado, citizens of Louisville were looking ahead. As the city recovered and rebuilt, the dream for a Children's Free Hospital took hold and endured. Today, Louisville has long recovered from the terrible storm in March of 1890, but the city still looks ahead. The Children's Free Hospital, renamed Kosair Children's Hospital in 1969, still operates as the only full-service hospital in Kentucky dedicated solely to the care of children. Ninety-six years later, in 1986, a state-of-the art pediatric facility opened expanding Kosair Children's Hospital services to include neonatal intensive care, pediatric trauma, and cardiology/cardiovascular surgery, marking another milestone for the former Children's Free Hospital.

THE LAST PIONEER SETTLEMENT

- 1904 -

Bell County

HIGH ON A 3,000-FOOT RIDGE IN BELL COUNTY, Kentucky, in isolated splendor, sat Hensley Settlement. Burton "Gabby Burt" Hensley Sr. had been led to the area by his mountain spirit after becoming disenchanted by the growing steel industry in the nearby town of Middlesboro. In 1903 Gabby Burt bought 500 acres on the high plateau, which he subdivided into sixteen parcels and distributed among his family members. Gabby Burt had used the land primarily for his cattle, but now, in the 1920s, the settlement was a beehive of activity. Farming, hunting, trading, raising livestock, and making moonshine occupied most of the inhabitants of this true pioneer settlement on Brush Mountain.

Hensley was not the first to inhabit the ridge. Before the Civil War, fugitive slaves seeking refuge had come to the mountaintop, as had squatters and hilltop farmers. But Hensley's purchase of the 500 acres changed the plateau into more than a pit stop on the way to somewhere else. One of his sons-in-law, Sherman Hensley, loved living there so much that he soon purchased an 38-acre plot, which he added to the 21 acres his wife, Nice Ann, had received from her father, Gabby Burt. In 1904, Sherman moved his family into the mountain home of a long-gone resident and continued clearing the land for farming and cattle grazing. Over the years, Sherman's family grew to nineteen children, who continued to live on the mountain after they married, raising their families there. As the Hensley family grew, other families moved off the mountain and eventually the settlement was entirely made up of members of the Hensley family tree. At one time, about one hundred people lived in the settlement.

This remote mountain plateau offered all the necessities a self-sufficient pioneer family needed to build a life. Forests teemed with pine and chestnut trees. Fertile land and wildlife to hunt and trap were as plentiful as they had been for the pioneers who traveled here 125 years earlier. Hensley settlers built four-room mud-chinked cabins whose hand-hewn floorboards were often nicked by a chopping ax. The settlers also built barns, assorted outbuildings, two water-powered mills, a cane mill, and blacksmith shop. Altogether, there were more than forty buildings in the settlement. In the fall after the crops were planted, the settlers continued to clear the land using a mattock and ax. Clearing land was made somewhat easier by an interesting technique the men used: They would cut rings around the trunks of large trees four years before they felled the trees, causing them to die before the men attempted to cut them down. On the cleared land, the settlers cultivated potatoes and fruit trees, as well as local ginseng. Young men often hired out to neighboring farmers, doing odd jobs such as shoe repair, harvesting, planting, or tending livestock.

While good honest work took up most of their time, another occupation—making moonshine—added to their coffers. Old and young men alike operated stills. In a small still, one man could make almost twenty-five gallons of liquor with one batch of distilling corn grain. This powerful moonshine was then transported down the mountain, fetching the good price of $10 per gallon. Since Hensley Settlement was so isolated and the road, which was more like a trail, up to the mountains was so rugged and treacherous, public officials rarely checked on these illegal operations and moonshine production flourished.

The settlers usually had cash on hand to buy the few modern conveniences they needed or wanted. They liked store-bought shoes, as well as cast-iron cook stoves, foot-powered sewing machines, windup Victrolas, and some families even had battery-powered radios. However, most food, clothing, tools, furniture, toys, medicine, musical instruments, and linens were handcrafted. Because they were so busy the only time settlers left the mountain was to purchase the goods they could not produce themselves, to mill corn meal, or to trade at market. Perhaps once a week Hensley men would travel down the mountain for mail and trade, and, a few times a year, to vote. Hensley women made the trip about every six weeks to buy groceries. The children, however, did not leave the mountain until age sixteen or eighteen, too busy farming, planting, hunting, or moving livestock across mountain lowlands.

Trips up and down the mountain required carrying heavy loads—either goods to trade in town or items purchased there. Particularly heavy were the sacks of grain needed for the moonshine operations. It was not uncommon for the men to carry 150 pounds up the mountain trails. In fact, the rite of passage to manhood centered on the amount of grain a boy could carry.

One of the favorite trips off the mountain for the Hensley men was Trade Day. Held once a month, the men would gather on a Friday evening and travel down the mountain into the valley with a stockpile of goods loaded onto mules and horses. There they would camp overnight and prepare for the next day's town trading. Early Saturday morning the bargaining for guns, watches, horses, and mules would start fast and furious. Their livestock was particularly sought after. It was not uncommon for bargaining to shift back and forth more than two dozen times throughout the day since the Hensley pioneers were known to be skilled negotiators.

Though Hensley settlers preferred remoteness from the outside world, they were still determined to educate their children. In 1913, Sherman Hensley and Willie Gibbons visited the Bell County school superintendent and asked that a teacher be sent to their mountaintop. The superintendent instructed the men they would need a schoolhouse before a teacher would be transferred up the mountain. Willie Gibbons spent forty of his own dollars and constructed a log building so that the Bell County school district could begin assigning teachers. Teachers lived and boarded in various homes on the settlement. Teachers usually stayed on the mountain for two to three weeks at a time. At times there were no teachers assigned to the mountain, so the Hensley women took turns teaching. By 1925, more than forty children were enrolled at the Brush Mountain School primary grade school, although few children stayed in school after the fourth grade. Most parents didn't think their children needed to have more than basic reading, writing, and math skills, and when they were about nine years old, they were taken out of school so they could work.

Out of necessity as well as desire, community life was simple and reflected a true communal spirit. The social high point of the year was Decoration Day, which took place the third Sunday in June every year. Everyone would assemble at the Hensley Cemetery and decorate graves with wild laurel, ivy, and honeysuckle. Hensley settlers took pride in the neatness of the cemetery, where thirty-seven head- and footstones indicated those laid to rest. The only two stones that had names marked on them belonged to Nice Ann and Gibbons Hensley. Decoration Day was also a time to celebrate or acknowledge all the marriages, baptisms, and funerals of the past year. Methodist, Primitive Baptists, and Dunkards (now United Brethern) ministers often visited Hensley Settlement preaching lengthy sermons in the hopes of making up for church services not held on a regular basis.

Life in the settlement was not easy and illness was not uncommon. The settlement experienced high child mortality rates. Sherman Hensley had three children buried on the mountaintop, two of whom were young married women who had succumbed to tuberculosis. When residents became sick, midwives administered herbal remedies. Balm was used to relieve colds and flu symptoms, calamint for fever, and fern root for boils. Catnip, sage, sweet basil, pennyrile, and red pepper tea (reportedly so spicy it felt as if the flesh was burning in one's throat) were common home remedies. Some home remedies were as dangerous as the disease or medical problem itself. Such was the case for Lige Hensley, who had been bitten by a rattlesnake. Kerosene (believed to kill snake poison) was poured onto his wound. Unfortunately, he began to hemorrhage at the mouth two or three days after his "treatment." Amazingly, he recovered both from the snakebite and the kerosene treatment. When herbal and home remedies did not work, or if the situation became dire, the Hensley settlers headed to the medical facilities located in the neighboring settlement of Middleboro. Even though they felt lucky to be relatively close to medical treatment, traveling to Middleboro was a long three to four mile mountainous trek via sled or horse for someone who was ill.

High in Bell County on Brush Mountain, life changed very little between Burton Hensley's arrival in 1903 and the start of World War II. However, by the end of WWII, the Hensley men who had left to serve in the military found it difficult to return to the pioneer way of life, especially with young brides in tow. Slowly but surely, the settlement lost many of its residents to the coalmines or public service jobs, which offered steady employment and regular income. When the Brush Mountain School closed in 1947, only four students remained (children of the three remaining Hensley Settlement families). Two years later, Sherman Hensley became the mountaintop's only occupant. Sadly, the settlement's first resident—and last—finally left the mountain in 1951. In 1959, Sherman Hensley sold his land to the Cumberland Gap National Historical Park, which had been slowly acquiring the surrounding land for the newly created National Park Service. Today, the remaining twenty-eight buildings have been painstakingly restored to their nineteenth-century conditions as a living museum and a testimony to the spirit and grit of one pioneer family.

DEVASTATING DROUGHT

- 1930 -

LOOKING BACK, THE PEOPLE IN THE NORTHERN COUNTIES of Kentucky saw the first signs of drought in June of 1930. The town of Dayton reported that no homes or businesses had water during a four-hour period. Likewise, neighboring Fort Thomas and Bellevue reported extremely low water pressure. Campbell County had to haul in water from the nearby cities of Newport and Alexandria. Local officials attributed the problem to residents over-watering their lawns and quickly imposed water rationing. At the grocery store and over back-yard fences, the topic of almost all conversations centered on burnt yards and low water supplies.

Even the water supply for river towns would have been severely depleted had it not been for the system of locks and dams along the Ohio and Kentucky Rivers. (Locks, which are rather like bathtubs, use gravity to raise the water level in a lock chamber and allow boats to move through areas of a river that would normally be impassable due to shallow water.) The Ohio River between Cincinnati and Covington measured only 3 feet deep. Water level for many Kentucky rivers became so low that production at hydroelectric power plants ceased.

In addition, railroads were forced to reduce shipping rates for grain, hay, and other supplies needed by farmers within affected areas because farmers had limited income due to poor crop or cattle yields. This was a nerve-wracking decision for the railroads, as well as several manufacturing industries (already trying hard to stay afloat on the heels of the stock market crash of 1929) that made similar cuts.

Nothing in the early months of 1930 foreshadowed the impending crises. In fact, the New Year began with fairly mild temperatures and above normal rainfall. February 1930 was noted as one of the warmest on record. Clover, grass, and winter grains like wheat began to grow more than two months ahead of the season. Farmers took advantage of the unseasonably spring-like weather by planting potatoes and tobacco. Kentucky rests in the middle latitude within the interior of the United States offering a moderate climate. January's average temperatures range from 29 degrees Fahrenheit in its most northern counties to 36 degrees in its southern counties. In 1930, the U.S. Weather Bureau reported normal temperatures averaging 45 degrees with normal record of rainfall (3½ inches) statewide. Snowfall was light: Total snowfall ranged from flurries in western counties to 1½ inches in the eastern portion of the state.

The only hint of a possible climatic twist was an occurrence of fluctuating extreme temperatures over a short time: On February 16 it was 2 degrees at Berea and 80 degrees at nearby Beaver Dam just nine days later. Starting in late February of 1930, the weather pattern became noticeably warmer and drier than normal. In the southern portion of the state, fewer than two inches of precipitation fell in Bowling Green in March and April. As a precursor of things to come, the daily high temperature reached 92 degrees on April 11, the first of three consecutive days at 90 degrees or above. The month of May brought more than three inches of rain and gave Bowling Green farmers some hope for their crops.

However, the brief spell of showers in mid-May did little to relieve the parched subterranean soil. Precipitation remained well below normal, and above normal temperatures baked the dry earth. Higher temperatures exacerbated drought effects because evaporation rates increased as the temperature soared. Moreover, there was no water draining from Kentucky's rolling plateaus or mountain ranges to the underlying outlets. With no flowing streams, creeks, and springs, thirsting cattle began to overgraze scorched rye and bluegrass pastures in search of the moisture typically found in plants. Without abundant corn cribs, many farmers either resorted to cutting their half-grown corn stalks to feed cattle or they sought assistance from the American Red Cross, which was trying to stretch its minimal feed and hay resources as far as possible. As a result of the lack of adequate feed or water for their animals, some farmers, who would have brought 100 head of cattle for sale in a single summer day, brought up to 10,000 head to try to gain some share of their value before starvation took its toll.

The crisis peaked along with the July temperatures. Northern Kentucky newspapers reported temperatures hitting 100 degrees on July 20, with nighttime temperatures falling only to an oppressive 92 degrees by 10:00 P.M. There was no measurable rainfall in Mayfield as temperatures soared to 100 degrees. Brush fires spontaneously erupted, prompting Campbell County officials to requisition water-hauling trucks from the Fort Thomas Army post. The Williamstown water system began selling water to farmers at a rate of fifty truckloads per day. Farmers resorted to dynamiting creeks and springs with hopes of locating more water. With most of the available water being used for agricultural purposes, many homes were unable to use water for life's "luxuries," such as bathing. In fact, Covington public health officials issued warnings for people not to bathe in pools or ponds since the stagnant water can carry typhoid. To add insult to injury, many people sought relief from the staggering heat by swimming in rivers and lakes, which resulted in an unusually high number of drowning deaths.

On July 26, thunderstorms erupted in Kenton and Campbell counties, but with temperatures still hovering at 100 degrees, any rainfall quickly evaporated. By late summer, corn crops were permanently lost. As for the cattlemen, the starvation of their herds wasn't the only problem they faced. Eight cows from Paul Rust's Campbell County farm died in August from a dangerous drought-resistant fungus that grew in the tall fescue. The effects of the drought on the cattle industry continued long after the drought ended. Cattle selling for $5.90 per hundredweight in 1925 sold for $3.05 eight years later.

Early in the summer, many farmers thought their tobacco crops could be salvaged if any rain fell over the next few weeks. However, as time passed and weather forecasters still were predicting no rain for August, some farmers resorted to harvesting their tobacco early. Officials in Lexington took matters into their own hands: They built a water pipeline running six miles to the Kentucky River.

While the drought was incredibly damaging across the entire region, Kentucky and Arkansas bore the brunt of Mother Nature's dry wit. Kentucky's cotton and tobacco sharecroppers were among the hardest hit. While more than $45 million of federal aid had been pledged for drought relief, the notion of government aid was hardly reassuring to the already indebted sharecroppers. Such aid came in the form of government loans backed by first mortgages on crops harvested in the fall, which meant that a portion of the crop yields were used as collateral. However, most cotton and tobacco tenant farmers had already borrowed from their landlords for seed and feed in the spring, when initial plantings began, leaving no money for food and clothing. By late summer, tenant farmers were unable to pay their landlords, who consequently were heavily mortgaged and unable to pay taxes. Many farmers resorted to seeking assistance from the Red Cross for food and supplies. The Red Cross fed, clothed, and supplied resources to 80,000 Kentuckians, a remarkable fact made even more remarkable given that the agency was short of resources after the Mississippi River flood three years earlier.

At last, in September, rain showers began to fall. Enough rain came to fill small cisterns and shallow creek beds, but the meager rains did nothing to restore municipal water supplies. Much to the relief of the farmers, the fall harvest of tobacco produced a fair yield, which helped in a small way to compensate for the devastated corn, alfalfa, and soybean crops. Crop losses totaled up to $85 million in Kentucky alone, not including cattle losses caused by forced sales that set low price records. Even with the light rains in September, the subsoil remained arid, which limited the fall plowing to only those patches of ground that were moist.

Even by October, the state saw little drought relief. Moreover, temperatures continued to fluctuate wildly. For example, on October 12, Bowling Green recorded a temperature of 94 degrees, compared to its normal temperature of 55 degrees, while just four days later Quicksand reported a chilly high of 16 degrees, when the average temperature for the day was typically 68 degrees. A mid-month frost killed the remaining dehydrated crops of potato, tomato, rye, and bluegrass. The situation was also dire for people not involved in agriculture. The University of Kentucky threatened to close its doors in mid-October, prompted by complaints of high water use by students. Lexington's situation grew progressively worse as well, and by December 1930 reports of near-famine circulated.

The drought came to an end by October 1931 but the devastation still took its toll. Eighty-six out of Kentucky's 120 counties applied for disaster relief. The Red Cross assisted families in more than 700 counties scattered throughout fourteen states in the nation's Midwest and South. More than 250,000 Kentuckians did not receive charitable aid or relief and were left to pick up the pieces of their lives as best they could.

THE OPENING OF LOUISVILLE
MUNICIPAL COLLEGE

- 1931 -

Louisville

EIGHTY-THREE BLACK STUDENTS WALKED THROUGH the doors of the Louisville Municipal College when it opened on February 9, 1931. Once inside, they found that the faculty consisted of seven teachers—one professor, one assistant professor, and five instructors. Students attended classes, which were only held during the day, in three buildings, which had once been the core campus of the now defunct Simmons University. In 1930 Louisville Municipal College had purchased the Simmons University property, renovated its buildings, and purchased curriculum materials for the nominal price of $145,000. The dean of the newly created Municipal College was Dr. Rufus Early Clement, a native Louisvillian who, when he was a student at Northwestern University in Chicago, had taken classes from Raymond A. Kent, who became the president of the University of Louisville in 1929.

Incisive and pinned as a man with an aggressive mind, Raymond Kent's proposals to the university's board of trustees were never once voted down during the first eight years of his presidency. Coming to the University of Louisville after six years as dean of Northwestern's College of Liberal Arts, Kent candidly remarked during his first few months in office that University of Louisville was "surprisingly good in some respects, disturbingly bad in others." He quipped, "at that time, the university as a whole, cut no figure in either the plans or consciousness of the city." Since accreditation and high academic standards were high on Kent's to-do list, he expected the same from its sister school, Municipal College. He was not disappointed after he hired Dr. Clement. Clement had served as dean of the history department at Livingstone College in Salisbury, North Carolina, for ten years and began his tenure at Municipal by hiring faculty capable of graduating undergraduate students within four years plus encouraging these graduates to seek postgraduate study.

At the time of its opening, Louisville Municipal College was one of only three African American municipal liberal arts colleges in the entire United States. However, Municipal College differed from its counterparts in Houston and Little Rock, which were both formed within the public school system and were under the jurisdiction of their respective boards of education. By contrast, Municipal College maintained its own campus, received jurisdiction from the University of Louisville board of trustees, and fell administratively under the responsibility of the university president. Functioning as "a separate institution under the administration of the board of trustees of the University of Louisville," it was the only full-fledged black liberal arts college in Kentucky and the only one in the nation supported by city funds.

Fortunately for Municipal College, Raymond Kent insisted on a rigorous educational program for the university and its related institutions. Because of this, the Committee on Accredited Relations of the University of Kentucky accredited Municipal College's first semester curriculum. The Municipal College offered both Bachelor of Science and Bachelor of Arts degrees that paralleled the liberal arts curriculum for white students who attended the University of Louisville. These stringent standards proved beneficial for Municipal College students, and by the time the college celebrated its tenth anniversary, nearly one third of its 1941 graduating class went on to pursue graduate and doctorate degrees at prestigious schools across the nation, including Howard University, Columbia University, the University of Michigan, and the University of Chicago.

The history of Municipal College dated back to 1879 when State University, later Simmons University, was founded to educate African American professionals. Its affiliation with the University of Louisville came much later. In 1920, expansion problems forced the University of Louisville to seek a $1 million bond referendum from voters to acquire additional grounds and remodel several buildings. A coalition of black and white activists, which included the Louisville Urban League, proposed the bond contain a provision for the funding of Negro higher education. This proposal was quickly denied by the University of Louisville board of trustees. The board used as their rationale the fact that state law prohibited the spending of any bond appropriations for any purpose other than those approved by the voters. Since funding for higher education for blacks was not in the original bond proposal, it could not be added now. A university board member then noted that there were no black applicants for higher education anyway. A committee member countered that indeed blacks had applied for university entrance but were denied because of race. Coalition members also pointed out that black teachers in the

Louisville public school system were forced to leave the city and seek higher education elsewhere, in contrast to white teachers who took courses at local universities and colleges.

Banding together, black Louisvillians rejected the $1 million University of Louisville bond issue, leading to its defeat at the polls. Five years later, with assurances of financial support for black higher education, a similar bond issue to ease University of Louisville's financial situation passed in 1925 and $100,000 was earmarked for black higher education. Over the next four years, coalition committee members pressed the university for building blueprints and timetables, but the estimated costs for construction were projected to run over university budget so promises went unanswered. And with the death of university president A. Y. Ford, the promise for local higher education for blacks came to a complete standstill.

By the summer of 1929, exasperated black leaders implored the newly arrived university president, Raymond A. Kent, to act. However, starting a black college was not high on Kent's priority list. Instead, Kent assumed the role of expanding and strengthening accreditation for the university's School of Law, as well as improving the "deadening apathy toward the university on the part of most Louisvillians." Finally, in 1929, a suggestion was made to the university board to purchase Simmons University, which was threatened with foreclosure. The following year, the University of Louisville purchased Simmons University for a mere $145,000, changing its name to Louisville Municipal College and instituting it as a liberal arts school for blacks.

Both university leaders and black community leaders were determined that Municipal College would offer a sound four-year undergraduate liberal arts program that would parallel the university's liberal arts college. Within four years, the college added an education degree, later followed by library science and social work degrees. In 1936, Municipal College was accorded full accreditation by the Southern Association of Colleges and Secondary Schools, thereby offering its graduates the ability to be admitted into some prestigious graduate programs throughout the nation. This accreditation proved its worth: Enrollment escalated from the initial 83 to 437 students by its fifth year.

The Depression hardly diminished Municipal College's growth; instead, it seemed to advance its goals. The Federal Emergency Relief Administration (FERA) allocated financial aid to nineteen students during the 1934-1935 terms. The FERA also offered office space for the adult education program. When the former Simmons University moved to its new site in downtown Louisville, the university failed to purchase several tracts of land between the old and new sites. Municipal College's board of trustees kept their eyes on this land, and in April 1936, the General Education Board appropriated $7,500 for Municipal College to purchase these parcels in light of the fact that the University of Louisville had recently spent $10,200 to purchase adjoining land and houses for its expansion. Municipal College was on the rise for ten more years.

However, following World War II, several factors led to the closing of Louisville Municipal College and its absorption into the University of Louisville. At the top of the list of factors was the high cost of running two separate liberal arts colleges. Furthermore, legal barriers to racial integration were being challenged successfully in the courts, and local private colleges were desegregating. In April 1950, university trustees approved closing the college and terminating its faculty. Despite backlash, staff and non-tenured faculty were given severance pay, three tenured faculty members received employment assistance, and one faculty member, Dr. C. H. Parrish Jr., became the first black faculty member in the University of Louisville's Sociology Department in 1951.

The Louisville Municipal College had served its students well for nineteen years, providing them with educational opportunities and unlocking new doors. The old doctrine of "separate but equal" had come to an end. The doors of public schools could no longer be closed to a person based on race, and students across the country were ready to walk through them.

FLOODWATERS SUBMERGE LOUISVILLE

- 1937 -

Louisville

"CALLING ALL BOATS! CALLING ALL BOATS! Go to Brook and First Street. Go to Brook and First Street. Take Dr. Dougherty to City Hospital. Take Dr. Dougherty to City Hospital."

"Calling all police! Calling all police! Looters reported on Chestnut Street. Looters reported on Chestnut Street. Police headquarter orders are to shoot to kill. Orders are shoot to kill."

More than 16,500 transmissions just like these, including many pleas for help, were transmitted during a two-week period in January 1937 when Louisville suffered the worst flood in its history. From January 24 to February 6, Louisvillians were cut off from the outside world and had to rely solely on the kindness and ingenuity of their neighbors as they figured out how to stay alive and eventually pick up the pieces of their town.

The danger to Louisville began when December's mild weather, with above-average rainfall, started to cause alarm in upstream cities in western Pennsylvania, where citizens watched the Allegheny, Monongahela, and Ohio Rivers start to rise. Soon, the Monongahela River flooded many towns in West Virginia, and the Ohio River inundated river towns along its banks, including Cincinnati, where one-fifth of the city was covered by the floodwaters. As the swollen Ohio River moved downstream, the Kentucky River slowly inundated more than half of the city of Frankfort and threatened the Kentucky State Prison. Kentucky Governor Al Chandler realized the dire circumstances at the prison and eventually called for the evacuation of the 2,900 inmates. However, before this occurred, lack of gas and electricity trapped inmates within their cells. Over the course of twenty-four hours, a mob scene unfolded when prisoners panicked as they watched the floodwaters reach a foot deep within the building and prison yard. Guards witnessed close to two dozen men risk the chance of being shot and jump into the Kentucky River. Realizing their motive was not to escape from punishment but to save their lives, one prison warden remarked, "we could have shot them down like rats in the water if we wanted to." But it wasn't necessary because the frigid river water froze any inmate's dreams of escape, and the escapees were quickly rounded up.

Louisvillians, accustomed to cyclical Ohio River flooding, heard the bulletins about flooding upstream and braced for their turn, never anticipating they would bear the brunt of the flooding. Kentucky had already recorded 15.77 inches of precipitation in January, which was eleven inches above normal, and two inches of snow covered the saturated ground when floodwaters spilled into the West End, a low-lying neighborhood adjacent to the Ohio River. Residents began to evacuate the West End as quickly as they could. The situation became even worse when Beargrass Creek, located in the East End, overflowed its banks, forcing water to backup into the sewer system. The floodwaters even extended to areas never before flooded, such as Churchill Downs, the famous racetrack located in south Louisville, more than five miles from the river. By this time, all points west, south, and east of the city were under floodwaters.

Schools closed and Louisvillians were instructed to stay home as torrential water gushed into buildings in Louisville's central business district. Strong currents and eddies made it impossible for the more than 175,000 residents attempting to flee toward higher ground on the other side of town to reach safety. In an effort to help those left stranded, more than 250 men built a long pontoon bridge made of empty whiskey barrels over Beargrass Creek to help evacuees escape from the West End. Railroads and armored trucks from Fort Knox also provided transportation for refugees.

By Sunday January 24, seventy percent of Louisville was flooded and the city had lost all electricity, water, and gas services. The city's main thoroughfare resembled whitewater rapids. City Hall and the County Courthouse became a virtual island where some sought shelter. Beargrass Creek was flowing backwards up into low-lying East End areas of Crescent Hill and the Highlands. The Waterside Electric plant was inundated with water and eventually had to be shut down. The lack of electricity meant the Neighborhood House canteen needed to use the high snow bank packed against the side of its building to refrigerate more than 400 pounds of pork, 40 gallons of beef stew, 300 pounds of spare-ribs, and sauerkraut. An early forerunner to the United Way, Neighborhood House was originally established to help turn-of-the-century immigrants assimilate into American culture, but now the facility was serving food and shelter to its own city residents. Seventy-five thousand refugees, more than 90 percent from the West End, were sent to the County Armory and still another 24,000 refugees were transported to either the tent colony in Algonquin Park, which had been set up for white citizens, or the camp for black citizens in George Rogers Clark Park.

Martial law was declared two days later just as evacuation of the West End concluded but meant little to the 20,000 residents who were still marooned downtown. As city gas and water services were shutdown, the residents who remained in their homes were left without any household services so garbage and refuse was thrown out of windows, leading to worse sanitary conditions and a filthy stench. Directed by City Hall, canoe, skiff, and powerboat rescuers attempted to order residents from their home, but most people refused to leave. For those who stayed behind, dubbed "river rats," boat rescuers became their only source for food and supplies. In fact, city officials often granted rescuers permission to break into grocery stores to obtain supplies that were certain to spoil. As the boats traveled around the area, some of the rescuers were bemused to find that residents wanted to merely bum cigarettes, take in a card game, or hop aboard one of the boats to go visit a relative down the street.

By Thursday, the Ohio River had crested at 57.1 feet, surpassing the old 1884 record by more than ten feet. A dredge boat commissioned by the Louisville Water Company began flushing out the submerged pump and eventually restoring drinking water to the East End. Neighborhood House canteen spooned out more than 50 gallons of soup, 60 gallons of coffee, and 1,000 cold cut sandwiches to truck drivers, boat rescuers, sand-bag crews, and City Hall workers. Neighborhood House was just one of several health agencies that dispensed tetanus inoculations during the crisis. Shifting all its resources into the Ohio River Valley, the Red Cross fed more than 270,000 Louisvillians and Jefferson County residents, estimating that they spent $700,000 on emergency relief.

As floodwaters slowly receded, the massive cleanup and assessment of damage began. When the Ohio River finally fell below flood stage on February 6, Louisville had tallied its property damage at more than $50 million. Sightseers clad in hip boots jumped aboard the Louisville & Nashville rail shuttle to see the flood aftermath. The muddied line surrounding Union Station's walls told of the flood's severity. Amazingly, however, the Jefferson County Medical Society reported only ninety fatalities with no reported cases of typhoid, diphtheria, or smallpox outbreaks, which were unusual statistics for a flood of such magnitude.

No doubt the Louisville communication system played a major role in mitigating many of the dire situations caused by the flood. The 16,500 "send-a-boat" transmissions and the continuous radio broadcasting by local stations of up-to-the-minute bulletins kept the public officials and citizens alike informed and ready for action. Although cut off from the outside world by floodwaters, Louisvillians knew what was taking place in their own city, and citizens there and across the nation listened intently as the drama unfolded.

KENTUCKY JOURNALIST NAMED
WOMAN OF THE YEAR

- 1976 -

Louisville

CAROL SUTTON COULD HARDLY BELIEVE HER ears and eyes. Her phone was ringing off the hook. There she was on the cover of *Time Magazine's* "1976 Women of the Year" issue. The feature article noted these women "arrived like a new immigrant wave in male America." Sutton shared the limelight and the honor, not to mention the cover photo, with First Lady Betty Ford, tennis star Billie Jean King, and the governor of Connecticut, Ella Grasso. And there among them was Carol Sutton, the managing editor of the *Louisville Courier-Journal*. Sutton was surprised that anyone should see her accomplishments on par with these women who were practically celebrities, but that kind of attitude was part of what had made her successful all these years. And successful she was—Sutton was the first female managing editor of a major United States newspaper.

Her promotion as the first female managing editor of a major U.S. newspaper two years earlier propelled her into the national limelight. Sutton remarked, "I'm not in any way a traditional, tough-talking managing editor. I don't go around banging shoes on desks or yelling at reporters across the city desk." Her colleagues agreed. *Courier-Journal* Sports columnist, Billy Reed, told *Time Magazine* that, "she handles copy better and has more imaginative story ideas than any other editor I've worked under." The path to recognition was not lined with roses but thanks in part to the emergence of the women's movement, female editors continued to push through the barriers found when working in the male-dominated publishing industry.

Sutton, a St. Louis native and former social worker, graduated from the University of Missouri in 1955. With her newly earned journalism degree in hand, she went to work for the *Louisville Courier-Journal.* Given that the year was 1955, she did not begin as a reporter but rather as secretary to the executive editor of the newspaper, James S. Pope Sr.—no doubt a more seemly job for a woman at the time. When she finally became a *Courier-Journal* reporter the following year, she was a city desk reporter, following everyone from City Hall candidates to the victims of the Eastern Kentucky flood. By 1963, Sutton was named editor of the *Women's World* section, then a compilation of food, fashion, furnishings, and family articles. Drawn toward human-interest stories, Sutton produced the "Cradles to Fame" series that profiled famous people born in Kentucky and some natives of neighboring states.

It was during these years that national daily newspaper women's pages began to undergo a radical shift. Newspapers were facing stiff competition from television, which prompted many newspapers to try to widen their readership. Newspaper editors realized they needed to attract more women readers, and since more than 40 percent of

American women worked outside the home, the women's pages of newspapers shifted from their original purpose of society news toward a reflection of the issues and trends most pertinent to working women. The transition posed concerns that advertisers, who had strongly supported women's pages (i.e., food, furniture, and fashion), may decide to take their advertising dollars elsewhere.

Sutton gleefully found herself in the right place at the right time and slowly began to transform the *Women's World* pages by printing more features and more investigative reporting. She surprised readers one Thanksgiving Day by presenting the first installment in a series on hunger in Kentucky. By 1972, Sutton changed the name of the section from *Women's World* to *Today's Living*, reasoning that current issues and problems were not solely women's issues. Her commitment to exposing inequities landed her the J.C. Penney–University of Missouri journalism award (an award created in 1960 to recognize and help improve women's pages) for an expose focusing upon fashion writers accepting gifts while covering the New York fashion scene, a practice considered unethical and akin to buying good press.

Sutton knew that "people stories" about families, children, rural issues, and travel were not merely lifestyle stories. Articles on these subjects often reflected important political and cultural facts about the country and, as such, belonged on the general news pages. Her flair for the human-interest story reflected back to her early pre-reporting years as a social worker for underprivileged children. "I got so caught up it was eating me up," remarked Sutton of her counseling days. "I just was suited for that." Ultimately she decided that social work was too emotionally draining, but she thoroughly enjoyed the ability to bring human-interest pieces to the front sections of the newspaper. Sutton often put stories written by city desk reporters in the *Today's Living* section, and her staffers would sometimes see their stories published in the general news pages. Sutton advocated the belief that activities by women should be newsworthy to both men and women and appointed a man as editor of *Today's Living* during her tenure.

Her appointment as managing editor in 1974 propelled Sutton into the national limelight. The year inaugurated many firsts: The same week Sutton was promoted to managing editor, Richard Nixon resigned the presidency. Also during her first year as managing editor, the Louisville and Jefferson County school systems merged and were ordered by a federal judge to implement a busing plan to achieve racial balance. Balanced and accurate reporting was important in keeping racial tensions under control. The *Courier-Journal* was successful in this endeavor. Under Sutton's leadership the paper won two national journalism awards, Sigma Delta Chi and Roy Howard, for public service for coverage of school desegregation. Photographic coverage of the busing crisis by the *Courier-Journal* and *The Louisville Times* won a Pulitzer Prize in 1976. The *Courier-Journal* was one of ten finalists for the Associated Press Managing Editors public-service award for its coverage of desegregation.

Sutton had an egalitarian vision of the role of newspapers that was central to her journalistic vision, and she credited the *Louisville Courier-Journal*'s dynamic environment for letting her pursue this vision. She summed up the newspaper's philosophy by simply saying, "We feel that women—both as readers and subjects of news—belong all through the newspaper, on the front page, in the regional news, in the sports section as well as in the features section." Sutton credited the feminist movement for "pushing newspapers to have a more rational view of people and their society and, therefore, of readers and their needs." She continued her egalitarian vision after she was named assistant to editor and publisher, Barry Bingham Jr. in 1976. In this position, she found that she had an even greater ability to pursue her belief that "your newspaper is one thing that really helps tie the state together and permit communication between east and west, urban and rural." More and more articles were written on all parts of the state, as well as stories pertinent to all genders and races. Also as senior editor, she actively recruited minority journalists, raising the percentage of black professionals on the news and opinion-page staffs from 3 percent to 10 percent over a five-year period. As a result of her work, the employment rate for black journalists in Louisville increased, and Sutton was honored to become the first white member of the National Association of Black Journalists.

Carol Sutton was recognized throughout the country as an important person in journalism. She was the discussion leader on ethics and on editing for the American Press Institute and chairper-son of the Pulitzer Prize juries in 1975 and 1976. Along with her work as committee member for Nieman Fellows in journalism at Harvard University, Sutton sat on the selection committee for Rhodes Scholars and was one of two women regents of the Associated Press Managing Editors.

Sutton's career was cut short when she died of cancer in February 1985. Carol Sutton was truly one of "A Dozen Who Made a Difference," just as *Time Magazine* reported in 1976. She made a difference to the world of journalism, as well as to the readers of the *Courier-Journal,* who were better informed about their world because of her.

PUBLIC OUTCRY FORCES
CLOSURE OF MAXEY FLATS

~ 1977 ~

Hillsboro

As early as 1972, former workers of the Maxey Flats Waste Disposal, a nuclear waste disposal facility located in Hillsboro, reported that "hot" liquid material was being "accidentally" dumped over the Fleming County hillside. After some investigation, the press reported that the liquid was plutonium-239 liquid waste, which was being recklessly spilled and was draining out of restricted areas. Rumors surfaced that contaminated tools, watches, and other small items, which were believed to have been buried, had actually been sold or given away. Shortly thereafter, local dairy farmers reported bizarre health problems afflicting their cattle, such as teeth grinding and skin depigmentation.

Alarmed by such reports, Fleming County residents formed the Maxey Flats Radiation Protection Association (MFRPA) in 1974 with the sole intention of closing Maxcy Flats. The group testified in front of the state's Special Advisory Committee on Nuclear Issues and stead-fastly secured a promise from the Kentucky governor that he would close the site "at the first evidence that nuclear waste could not be contained." The group further waged their battle in the national media.

The evidence that ultimately led to the closure of Maxey Flats surfaced in August 1977 when state-monitoring reports confirmed low-level radioactive waste was seeping from buried trenches. The Environmental Protection Agency (EPA) and the Kentucky Human Resources Department found plutonium isotopes more than 200 feet from the shallow unused trenches, with seepage occurring more quickly than previously believed. Although the amount of seepage indicated that the volume of contaminated liquids was very small, two significant details were revealed. First, the site's disposal techniques carelessly allowed rainwater to infiltrate the buried trenches, which in turn caused contaminated groundwater and surface water runoff to flow into the Rock Lick tributaries. Further studies were conducted by the EPA, the U.S. Nuclear Regulatory Agency, and the U.S. Geological Survey between the initial 1972 reports and 1977 closure. In December 1977, the MFRPA finally gained approval to close the site after evidence was brought forth that showed nuclear waste was not properly contained, ending three contentious years of struggle.

The closing of Maxey Flats initiated cleanup efforts as well as a stream of finger pointing. State officials admitted the site had been poorly chosen back in 1962. At the time, the site's diverse geology and above-average annual precipitation had seemed like good reasons to choose the site. When Maxey Flats began operation, waste disposal issues were of little concern. Many state officials were quite interested in bringing the nuclear industry to the state and more than willing to ignore the question of what to do with the waste the industry produced. It was believed by many state officials that nuclear energy could make Kentucky a major player in the emerging nuclear energy industry. Also, during those years considerable federal funding had been appropriated for nuclear research, but none for safe nuclear waste disposal.

In 1962, the Kentucky General Assembly passed a number of statutes that would allow a nuclear burial site to be located in Kentucky. Western Kentucky sites were eliminated due to earthquake risks. Sites in northeastern Kentucky were focused on due to their high shale deposit, which is water resistant. What was not given much thought, however, was the fact that geological changes over time result in shale developing cracks and fissures. After some debate, the state signed a twenty-five year lease with the Nuclear Engineering Company (NECO) for operation of a nuclear waste disposal site at Maxey Flats. The site was a parcel of 252 acres perched across a flat-topped ridge 380 feet above the surrounding Rock Lick valley. Ironically, the NECO's initial geologic survey indicated major problems with the site, namely the possibility that heavy rainfall could infiltrate buried trenches.

Maxey Flats started to bury toxic waste in May of 1963, but this activity drew very little public attention over the next nine years. More than 99 percent of Maxey Flats hazardous waste that contained cancer-causing radionuclides was brought from research laboratories, electric utilities, colleges, universities, government and health care centers, manufacturing companies, and nuclear power plants across the United States. Approximately 85 percent of the radioactive waste that was buried in trenches at Maxey Flats contained low-level contamination; the remainder was high-level wastes including plutonium, which is believed to be radiologically toxic for more than 25,000 years.

Since low-level waste is made up of various concentrations from spent nuclear fuel and reprocessed nuclear residues, its long-term radioactivity is questionable. In fact, controversy surrounds the question of whether or not low-level waste warrants disposal in shallow landfills. At Maxey Flats, 51 trenches measuring 650 feet long were filled with radioactive waste. Some refuse was buried in wooden crates, cardboard boxes, paper bags, or metal drums. Some material was just buried uncontained. In some instances, the waste was covered with as little as 5 inches of soil, in direct violation of the Nuclear Regulatory Commission's recommended 10 feet of soil, shale, or rock material.

Routine soil monitoring by the state in 1972 uncovered a dangerous situation. Plutonium was escaping from trenches through shale fissures and migrating through surface water run-off. These findings were turned over to the EPA, U.S. Nuclear Regulatory Agency, and U.S. Geological Survey, which resulted in increased public awareness of Maxey Flat's negligent burial practices. By 1976, public outcry forced the state General Assembly to impose an excise tax on further nuclear waste buried in the Commonwealth, but this action was the tip of the iceberg to remedy the problem.

NECO, in an attempt to switch media focus from its operations, charged that the EPA report did not conclusively show radioactive seepage or failed to indicate that measured radiation was below permissible levels. The state was assured that the site was not a public health threat; however, residents and officials were concerned by the lack of scientific evidence discussing the long-range implications of radioactive contamination. Questions remained as to how to prevent further water infiltration within buried trenches.

Over the years, almost 5 million cubic feet of radioactive material was buried at Maxey Flats, making it the largest commercial nuclear waste disposal facility in the nation. However, in the end, not a single nuclear research facility broke ground in Kentucky, disappointing those who had hoped to bring a new industry to Kentucky. A state supervisory committee recommended Kentucky retain ownership of the site in an effort to retain control for approving or disapproving the locating, opening, closing or reopening of a site or facility within the Maxey Flat borders.

Between 1978 and 1990, several remediation efforts were initiated, including injection of grout-like materials into the soil to create an impenetrable barrier. This method was abandoned in 1986 when studies confirmed the procedure produced hazardous tritium. That same year, the EPA placed Maxey Flats on its National Priorities List, making it eligible for Superfund maintenance and stabilization. (The EPA deems Superfund sites toxic waste areas. As a Superfund site, cleanup methods must permanently decrease the amount of waste and toxicity while protecting human health. There is at least one Superfund site in every state.) With the closure of Maxey Flats in 1977, the MFRPA felt confident the state and EPA were taking control of the situation and thus decided to disband. Nonetheless, former members of MFRPA continued their grassroots efforts by securing Technical Assistance Grants from the EPA to keep the public involved in decision-making at the local level for Superfund cleanup efforts.

In the meantime, events at Maxey Flats heightened the public's awareness of nuclear waste storage and management throughout the state and nation. In Kentucky, three articles of state legislation outlined standards for the state's future nuclear waste disposal. It was acknowledged in eight separate studies that Maxey Flats presented no significant public health hazard to residents living near the site. More disturbing was the fact that no independent expert was willing to give assurance for the potential long-term impact of radioactive contamination.

The EPA tracked down entities creating this type of toxic waste and by 1986 had issued notices of potential liability to nearly a hundred institutions, including many universities. The Comprehensive

Environmental Response, Compensation and Liability Act (CER-CLA) held institutions liable if their waste was disposed of at Maxey Flats. By 1995, the U.S. Department of Justice and EPA entered into a consent decree (an agreement sanctioned by a court) with 400 private and government parties to stabilize and minimize further pollution from Maxey Flats for a cost of an estimated $60 million. Under one decree, 43 companies were ordered to remove approximately 3 million gallons of wastewater buried in trenches and install an interim cap. Six federal agencies paid for a majority of the $45 million work.

Remedial design and action to cleanup the site consists of two major areas: 1) leachate (radioactive contaminated trench water) removal and disposal, and 2) capping restricted area plus soil and erosion control. Reinforced concrete bunkers (for disposal of solidified radioactive leachate and other contaminated materials) were completed. Approximately 900,000 gallons of leachate were removed from within the landfill since current dewatering operations began in September 1998. Construction of a sixty-acre synthetic interim cap and associated surface water and erosion control ended in 2002. Remediation costs Kentucky taxpayers close to $1 million annually. The state will implement an extended maintenance plan, which may last up to 100 years to allow natural stabilization before the final cap is constructed. In 2012, site maintenance, monitoring, and institutional control will revert to the state in perpetuity. Portions of the site will be restricted for land use for a minimum of 200 years.

OPERATION BOPTROT

- 1992 -

Louisville

THE WORDS "KENTUCKY," "HORSES," AND "RACING" seem synonymous in the minds of many, but unfortunately, in the 1990s the terms "payoff" and "bribes" were equally linked with the bluegrass image many Kentuckians had of their state. In 1992, an FBI investigation began to unfold and would ultimately lead to convictions and jail time for some of Kentucky's leading politicians. There had long been suspicion that ethical considerations were relegated to the back burner when laws concerning horse racing came before the Kentucky General Assembly. It was for this allegation that the FBI opened their investigations into BOPTROT. BOP stood for the horse racing legislative committee (Business, Organizations, and Professions Committee) and TROT was used to signify the harness racing industry.

The BOPTROT investigation and eventual sting operation began in September 1990 when Riverside Downs harness racetrack owner, M. L. Vaughn, feared he was facing bankruptcy. He phoned then Senate Majority Whip, Helen Garrett, to discuss the negative ramifications of a 1988 state law granting rival thoroughbred racetrack, Ellis Park, rights to conduct lucrative intertrack wagering on races telecast from other tracks.

A simulcast is a broadcast of a horserace that allows wagering between two or more sites. During the broadcast of the race, wagers are transmitted to a central betting site that facilitates both a large betting pool and the actual broadcast of the horserace. Simulcast fuels interest in smaller racetracks, allowing them to televise and conduct off-track betting on races occurring anywhere in the state and nation. This is a crucial way for smaller tracks to attract viewers and thus potential betters away from more lucrative racing venues, such as at thoroughbred racing tracks. Simulcast dates, similar to live race dates, are granted to individual tracks by the state racing commission. In areas where multiple tracks operate, the policy had traditionally been to split simulcast dates between the facilities. However, the 1988 state law would cut Riverside Downs out of the action, thus plunging Riverside Downs into bankruptcy.

Riverside Downs was lobbying to have the law reconsidered in a special legislative session in early 1991. Opposition to the law included the state attorney general, who felt the law was unconstitutional. Helen Garrett, well aware of the impact of the horse racing industry to the state's economy, assured Vaughn the situation could be remedied provided that Vaughn provide proceeds to the following recipients: $30,000 to the House, $40,000 to the Senate, etc. Vaughn was suspicious of Garrett's payoff and decided to contact the FBI. When Vaughn contacted Garrett again, she had lowered her earlier price to $2,000 for lobbying fees, but unbeknownst to her, the FBI was now involved. The FBI provided the funds, and Vaughn wrote the $2,000 check.

The FBI zeroed its investigation in on the Business, Organizations, and Professions (BOP) Committee that oversaw the horse racing industry. Vaughn, under FBI direction, approached outgoing BOP vice chairman, John Hall, concerning Riverside's dilemma. Hall suggested Vaughn mingle among other BOP committee members at an upcoming December 1990 trade convention in Las Vegas and further proposed that he (Hall) would unofficially lobby for Riverside Downs. This led to a perfect FBI setup. During the Jockey Guild convention in Las Vegas, FBI agents posing as Riverside Downs representatives hobnobbed among BOP committee members, including Hall, at private parties and blackjack tables. The undercover agents passed bribes to legislators to block the breed-to-breed bill banning state harness tracks from simulcasting thoroughbred races. Breed-to-breed is the opposite of cross breed competition (i.e., horse to horse racing versus dog to horse racing); allowing horse racing broadcast signals only into horse racing tracks, rather than dog racing tracks. Hall accepted $4,850 from an operative, the majority of which he claimed to pass to other legislators.

In early 1991, FBI agents accompanied by attorneys from the U.S. attorney's office swarmed Hall's Louisville office, unveiling incriminating photos, videos, and other evidence related to his bribe taking. Hall had two choices: cooperate with the FBI or spend time in jail. He chose the first option. Under the FBI's direction, Hall became instrumental in luring three key BOPTROT members, William McBee, Bruce Wilkinson (the nephew of then-Governor Wallace Wilkinson), and John "Jay" Spurrier, to fix an arbitration dispute for Riverside Downs in exchange for a $50,000 payoff from the track. In order to avoid an IRS audit, the ruse intended Hall to handle the exchange and declare the $50,000 as lobbying income and in return, he would keep $20,000 for his efforts. The rest would be split between Spurrier, McBee, and Wilkinson. The three men agreed to the deal, giving specific instructions to Hall to leave the money in a designated Frankfort hotel room.

On January 7, Hall delivered the wiretapped suitcase (filled with $30,000 worth of marked twenties) to room 418 at a Holiday Inn hotel. Once Hall deposited the suitcase in the room, he left the hotel to meet McBee at Flynn's, a local Frankfort restaurant. Upon his exit, Spurrier, who was hiding in the next hotel room, took the payoff and drove back to his condo. There, Spurrier and Wilkinson counted their shares, unwittingly under FBI surveillance. When Spurrier and Wilkinson left the condo, the FBI surrounded and arrested the pair. The coup was dramatic for the FBI, who had now snagged a key lobbyist in Operation BOPTROT. Faced with the same terms as Hall, Spurrier choose to work for the FBI sting versus serving prison time.

Spurrier, now an FBI operative, teamed with an unsuspecting McBee to kill the breed-to-breed bill on behalf of Riverside Downs. McBee had recently paid off targeted legislators $1,000 plus House BOP chairman, Jerry Bonger, a tidy sum of $2,000. FBI videotape also caught McBee slipping his best friend, House Speaker Don Blandford, a $500 "thank you" in return for the speaker's help blocking the bill. Blandford remarked, "Well, bless your heart," as he stuffed the money in his pocket. McBee said, "I share with my buddies."

On March 30, 1992, the FBI closed in on William McBee. McBee, not thrilled at the prospect of jail time, initially agreed to cooperate with the FBI investigation. However, unwilling to incriminate his cronies, McBee had a change of heart and leaked the news of the sting during a party honoring him as the "Kentucky Lobbyist of the Year." The FBI cover was blown wide open. They had to move quickly before McBee's friends had time to cover their tracks. The next day, March 31, thirty FBI agents flooded the Kentucky General Assembly floor, interviewing and issuing subpoenas to legislators for travel and campaign finance records. Operation

BOPTROT, the state's largest public wrongdoing investigation, jumped the track gate.

Within the next three years, twenty-one defendants would plead guilty to charges ranging from racketeering, fraud, extortion, and bribery, bringing down the former Speaker of the Kentucky House, the nephew of a former governor, and a handful of assorted lobbyists and public figures. No breed-to-breed legislation was ever filed. Ultimately, the most damaging evidence to unfold in the press was the early videotape of McBee slipping longtime House Speaker Don Blandford a $500 thank you.

Operation BOPTROT led to several successive ethics investigations. Among these was the 1993 trial of a former state auditor-turned-lobbyist, George Atkins, accused of paying a state legislator $10,000 in exchange for a crucial vote on a bill to allow Humana, the national medical insurance conglomerate, to expand operations at Louisville corporate headquarters. Additionally, a member of the Senate Banking Committee was convicted of conspiracy and attempted extortion for trying to recoup money he said was promised for his vote on a 1984 bill loosening state banking regulations. The BOPTROT crackdown even led a federal grand jury to investigate 1994 allegations that federal mine inspectors solicited bribes from Eastern Kentucky coal operators. By the time prosecutors officially ended Operation BOPTROT in 1995, the General Assembly had adopted stringent ethics restrictions and campaign finance reforms. Today, Kentucky, horses, and racing are still synonymous, but one hopes Operation BOPTROT closed the chapter on payoffs and bribes.

KENTUCKY FACTS AND TRIVIA

Kentucky covers 39,728 square miles with an estimated 101 persons per square mile.

Kentucky earned its name from an Indian word, *Kentucke,* whose possible meanings include *Land of Tomorrow* and *Meadowland.* It is one of four states officially called commonwealths. The others are Massachusetts, Pennsylvania, and Virginia. Kentucky was named a commonwealth to honor Virginia, which owned the region before Kentucky became a state.

Kentucky contains 120 counties and has 38 state senators and 100 state representatives.

Kentucky's state motto is *United We Stand, Divided We Fall.*

Kentucky has 938,750 acres of land in farms. As of 2003, there were 2,127 farms averaging 441 acres each.

The 2000 census reported Kentucky's population was 4,041,769. The state's population ranked 25th in the nation. The most recent 2003 census estimates the state population at 4,117,827. Over the three-year period, there has been a 1.9% increase.

Kentucky's top five largest industries by Gross State Product in 2001 were: 1) motor vehicles and equipment; 2) health services; 3) business services; 4) food and kindred products; and 5) electric, gas, and sanitary services.

The range of elevation in Kentucky is more than 3,500 feet. The lower elevations are at the western edge of Kentucky with elevations of about 400 feet above mean sea level and, to the east, Black Mountain rises to 4,139 feet above mean sea level.

The state's record low temperature was set January 19, 1994, in Shelbyville, when the temperature dropped to -37° F. The record high temperature was set July 28, 1930, in Greensburg at 114° F.

Kentucky gained statehood June 1, 1792, becoming the 15th state.

Frankfort has been Kentucky's capital since 1793. Lexington served as the temporary capital in 1792.

Kentucky's state song is *My Old Kentucky Home,* words and music by Stephen Collins Foster.

The Kentucky state bird is the Kentucky Cardinal.

The Kentucky state flower is the Goldenrod.

The 1982 Fancy Farm Picnic in Graves County was added to the *Guinness Book of World Records* in 1985 when it was recognized as the World's Largest Picnic. At the event, 6.8 tons of lamb, pork, and chicken were consumed.

The Mammoth-Flint Ridge cave system, located entirely within Kentucky, is the world's longest at more than 300 miles (483 kilometers). It includes the famous Mammoth Cave and is part of Mammoth Cave National Park.

The gold depository at Fort Knox contains more than $6 billion in gold bullion. The bullion represents nearly all of the gold owned by the U.S. government.

The Kentucky Derby is the oldest annual horse race in the United States. The first Derby was run in 1875 as part of the opening day program for Churchill Downs racetrack in Louisville.

The world's first free-flowing oil well was drilled near Burkesville in 1829. Before that, people sporadically recovered oil when it seeped through the ground or accidentally gushed from salt wells. The Burkesville oil was never collected; it flowed unused into the nearby Cumberland River.

Kentucky tobacco growers lead the world in the production of burley tobacco, which is the type of tobacco typically used in cigarettes. Kentucky has held this ranking for more than 100 years.

An oak tree stump encased in concrete and painted white in Fancy Farm bears a commemorative plaque stating, *"this tree trunk remains a symbol of the years since 1880 where political speeches were made on the first Saturday in August at the Fancy Farm annual picnic."* Cynics say the old oak died from the effects of the political promises that were told under its limbs over the course of 185 years.

BIBLIOGRAPHY

Discovery of a Mastodon Graveyard

Fenwick, Jason M. and Marcia K. Weinlard. *A Reconnaissance and Evaluation of Archaeological Sites in Boone County, Kentucky, No. 8.* Frankfort, Ky.: Kentucky Heritage Commission, 1978.

Lutes, Ann. *The Brief History of Boone County, Kentucky.* A Paper for the Boone County Historical Society, February 18, 1955, pp. 2–5.

Semonin, Paul. *American Monster.* New York: New York University Press, 2000.

Stevens, Sylvester K. and Donald H. Kent, eds. *The Expedition of Baron de Longueuil.* A Paper for the Erie County Historical Society, 1941. www.gbl.indiana.edu/archives/miamis8/M31-45_50a.html.

Warner, Jennifer S. *Boone County: From Mastodons to the Millennium.* Burlington, Ky.: The Committee, 1998, pp. 9–26.

The Expedition of Dr. Thomas Walker

Belue, Ted F. *The Hunters of Kentucky: A Narrative History of America's First Far West, 1750–1792.* Mechanicsburg, Pa.: Stackpole Books, 2003.

Burns, David M. *Gateway: Dr. Thomas Walker and the Opening of Kentucky.* Bell County Historical Society, 2000, pp. 21–52.

Clark, Thomas D. *Kentucky: Land of Contrast.* New York: Harper & Row, 1968.

Nyland, Keith R. *Doctor Thomas Walker (1715–1794) Explorer, Physician, Statesman, Surveyor and Planner of Virginia and Kentucky.* Ann Arbor, Mich.: University Microfilms International, 1977.

Tuggle, Kenneth H. "Dr. Thomas Walker Bicentennial Celebration." *The Filson Club History Quarterly,* 24, no. 3 (1950–1951), pp. 276–79.

Battle of Boonesborough

Chinn, Allie D. "Kentucky Became Fifteenth State of Federal Union in 1792 Following Long Fight," *Lexington Herald,* 21 July 1935.

Draper, Lyman C. and Ted F. Belue. *The Life of Daniel Boone.* Mechanicsburg, Pa.: Stackpole Books, 1998.

Faragher, John M. *Daniel Boone: The Life and Legend of an American Pioneer.* New York: Henry Holt & Company, 1992.

Lofaro, Michael A. *Daniel Boone: An American Life.* Lexington, Ky.: University of Kentucky Press, 2003.

Toomey, Michael A. "Daniel Boone 1734–1820," *The Tennessee Encyclopedia of History and Culture,* Carrol Van West, editor-in-chief. Knoxville, Tennessee, 1998.

Jenny Wiley's Indian Captivity

Connelley, William E. *History of Kentucky: The Founding of Harman's Station With An Account of the Indian Captivity of Mrs. Jennie Wiley and the Exploration & Settlement of the Big Sandy Valley in the Virginias and Kentucky.* New York: Torch Press, 1910.

Ely, William. *The Big Sandy Valley: A History of the People and Country From the Earliest Settlement to the Present Time.* Baltimore: Genealogical Publishing Company, 1969.

Hall, Mitchel. *Johnson County Kentucky: A History of the County and Genealogy of Its People Up to 1927.* Louisville, Ky.: Standard Press, 1928.

Smith, J. K. "Jenny Wiley, Pioneer, Wife and Mother." *The Kentucky Club Woman* 55, no. 5 (1970), pp. 8–9.

Cane Ridge Revival

Boles, John B. *The Great Revival: Beginnings of the Bible Belt.* Lexington, Ky.: University Press of Kentucky, 1972.

Coleman, J. Winston. *Kentucky: A Pictorial History.* Lexington, Ky.: University Press of Kentucky, 1971.

Conkin, Paul K. *Cane Ridge: America's Pentecost.* Madison, Wis.: University of Wisconsin Press, 1990.

Eslinger, Ellen. "Some Notes on the History of Cane Ridge Prior to The Great Revival." *The Register of the Kentucky Historical Society* 91, no. 1 (1993), pp. 1–23.

Shaw, Wayne. "The Historians' Treatment of the Cane Ridge Revival." *The Filson Club History Quarterly* 37, no. 3 (1963), pp. 249–53.

Towns, Elmer and Douglas Porter. *The Ten Greatest Revivals Ever: From Pentecost to the Present.* Ann Arbor, Mich.: Servant Publications, 2000.

The Establishment of the Pleasant Hill Shaker Colony

Hutton, Daniel Mac-Hir. *Old Shakertown and the Shakers.* 5th ed. Harrodsburg, Ky.: Harrodsburg Herald Press, 1936.

Merton, Thomas. *Seeking Paradise: The Spirit of the Shakers.* Maryknoll, N.Y.: Orbis Books, 2003.

Morse, Flo. *The Story of the Shakers.* Woodstock, Vt.: Countryman Press, 1986.

Neal, Julia. *The Kentucky Shakers.* Lexington, Ky.: University Press of Kentucky, 1982.

Thomas, Samuel W. and Mary L. Young. "The Development of Shakertown at Pleasant Hill, Kentucky." *The Filson Club History Quarterly* 49, issue 3 (1975), pp. 231–55.

Frontier Abdominal Surgery

Flexner, James T. *Doctors on Horseback: Pioneers of American Medicine.* New York: Fordham University Press, 1992.

Gray, Laman. *The Life and Times of Ephraim McDowell.* Louisville, Ky.: V. G. Reed, 1997.

"Operations Which Made State's Early Surgeons Famous Recalled," *Louisville Times,* 17 December 1923.

Schachner, August. *Ephraim McDowell "Father of Ovariotomy" and Founder of Abdominal Surgery.* Philadelphia: J. B. Lippincott Company, 1921.

Beauchamp–Sharp Tragedy

Coleman, J. Winston. *The Beauchamp–Sharp Tragedy.* Frankfort, Ky.: Roberts Printing Co., 1950.

Giles, James and Wanda Giles. "Robert Penn Warren." *Dictionary of Literary Biography 152: American Novelists since World War II,* 4th series (1995), pp. 282–97.

Goldhurst, William. "The New Revenge Tragedy: Comparative Treatments of the Beauchamp Case." *The Southern Literary Journal* 22, no. 1 (1989) pp. 117–27.

Jillson, Willard Rouse. "The Beauchamp–Sharp Tragedy in American Literature." *The Kentucky State Historical Society* 36, no. 114 (1938), pp. 54–59.

Snider, Pearl S. "Jereboam O. Beauchamp Was First To Be Legally Hanged in Kentucky." *The Kentucky Explorer* (May 1994), pp. 28–30.

Asiatic Cholera Finds a Hero

Baird, Nancy D. "Asiatic Cholera's First Visit to Kentucky: A Study in Panic and Fear." *The Filson Club History Quarterly* 48, no. 4, (1974), pp. 228–40.

Crawford, Byron, "Slave Stayed to Nurse Town in Epidemics," *The Louisville Courier-Journal,* 30 July 2004.

McDonald, Tom, "Springfield 'Hero:' Louis Sansbury and the Cholera Epidemics," *The Springfield Sun,* 28 July 2004.

Delia Webster's Excursion on the Underground Railroad

Crisler, Lois. "Lewis Hayden Says 'All Aboard,'" *Footsteps* 5, no.1 (Jan–Feb 2003), pp. 18–22.

Eisan, Frances K. *Saint or Demon? The Legendary Delia Webster Opposing Slavery.* New York: Pace University Press, 1998.

Field, Phyllis F. "Delia Webster and the Underground Railroad," *Civil War History* 43, no. 2 (June 1997), pp. 179–81.

Runyon, Randolph P. *Delia Webster and the Underground Railroad.* Lexington, Ky.: University Press of Kentucky, 1996.

A Governor Strives for Neutrality

Clift, C. Glenn. *Governors of Kentucky.* Cynthiana, Ky.: C. Glenn Clift, 1942.

Dues, Michael T. "Governor Beriah Magoffin of Kentucky: Sincere Neutral or Secret Secessionist?" *The Filson Club History Quarterly* 40, no. 1 (1966), pp. 22–27.

———. *Neither North Nor South: The Rhetoric of Confrontation, Compromise, and Reaction in Kentucky, 1833–1868.* Ann Arbor, Mich.: University Microfilms International, 1973.

———. "The Pro-Secessionist Governor of Kentucky: Beriah Magoffin's Credibility Gap." *Kentucky Historical Society Register* 67, no. 3 (1969), pp. 221–31.

Hutchinson, Jack T. *Bluegrass and Mountain Laurel: The Story of Kentucky in the Civil War.* A Paper for the Cincinnati Civil War Round Table, 2000.

Mulligan, William H. *The Civil War in the Jackson Purchase Region of Kentucky: A Survey of Historic Sites and Structures.* A Report for the Kentucky Heritage Council, 1996.

Civil War Refugees' Expulsion from Camp Nelson

Lucas, Marion. "Camp Nelson, Kentucky, During the Civil War: Cradle of Liberty or Refugee Death Camp?" *The Filson Club History Quarterly* 63, no. 4 (1989), pp. 439–52.

Sears, Richard. *Camp Nelson, Kentucky: A Civil War History.* Lexington, Ky.: University of Kentucky Press, 2002.

———. "John G. Fee, Camp Nelson, and Kentucky Blacks, 1864–1865." *Kentucky Historical Society Register* 85, no. 1 (1987), pp. 29–45.

The Creation of the Louisville Slugger

Cocanougher, Kelly. "Babe Ruth's Ghost May Still Watch How 'Sluggers' Are Made," *The Louisville Times,* 10 October 1977.

Hill, Bob. *Crack of the Bat: The Louisville Slugger Story.* Champaign, Ill.: Sports Publishing, 2000.

Mussill, Bernie. "The Evolution of the Baseball Bat . . . From the First Crack to the 'Clank.'" *Oldtyme Baseball News,* www.stevetheump.com/Bat_History.htm.

Von Borries, Philip. "Pete Browning: The Original Louisville Slugger." Black Book Partners, LLC, www.jockbio.com.

Louisville Tornado and Founding of the South's First Free Children's Hospital

Johnston, J. Stoddard. *Memorial History of Louisville: From Its First Settlement to the Year 1896.* Chicago: American Biographical Publishing, 1896.

Mellor, Gail McGowan. *Kosair Children's Hospital: A History 1892–1992.* Louisville, Ky.: Alliant Health System Publishing, 1992.

Yater, George H. "The Terrible-Tempered Tornado of 1890." *Louisville Magazine* 29, no. 3 (March 1978), pp. 34–35, 79–82.

The Last Pioneer Settlement

America's Last Pioneer Settlement. Lexington, Ky.: Eastern Kentucky Resource Development Project, University of Kentucky Cooperative Extension Service, 1964.

Cox, William E. *Hensley Settlement: A Mountain Community.* Philadelphia, Pa.: Eastern National Park and Monument Association, 1978.

Schroeder, Joan V. "Time Turned Backward: Kentucky's Hensley Settlement." *Blue Ridge Country: Exploring the Mountains of the South,* www.blueridgecountry.com.

Devastating Drought

Eschrich, J. L. "Drought: Kentucky." *The New Republic* 66, no. 38 (February 25, 1931), pp. 38–41.

Hill, Jerry. *Kentucky Weather.* Lexington, Ky.: University Press of Kentucky, 2005.

Kendall, James. "Climatological Data: Kentucky Section." *U.S. Department of Agriculture Weather Bureau* 35, no. 2–10 (1930).

Reis, Jim, "Decade of Destruction," *The Kentucky Post,* 8 June 1998.

Robbins, A. "Hunger-1931." *The Nation* 132, no. 3423 (February 11, 1931), pp. 151–53.

The Opening of Louisville Municipal College

Bond, Max, "Interracially Speaking," *The Louisville Herald,* 8 December 1929.

"Kent's First Decade Has Brought Results," *Louisville Courier-Journal,* 2 July 1939.

Ragland, John M. "Public Education for Louisville Negroes," *Louisville Courier-Journal,* 4 August 1928.

Wilson, George. *A Century of Negro Education in Louisville, Kentucky.* Louisville, Ky.: Louisville Municipal College, 1941.

Floodwaters Submerge Louisville

Breaux, Gustave. "1937 Flood at Louisville—And the French Named the Ohio 'La Belle Rivier,'" *The Filson Club History Quarterly* 11, no. 2 (1937), pp. 109–19.

The Flood: The Great 1937 Disaster. Wilkes-Barre, Pa.: Picture Press, 1937.

Hammon, Stratton. "Send A Boat: Images of Louisville's 1937 Flood." *Kentucky Historical Society Register* 81, no. 2 (1983), pp. 154–67.

Ingram, Frances. "Neighborhood House Feeds Thousands Daily," *The Neighborhood House Flood Story,* Louisville, Kentucky: Neighborhood House, 1937.

Yater, George. "A Flood of Memories: An Eyewitness Account of the 1937 Flood." *Louisville Magazine* 38, no. 1 (1987), pp. 42–45.

Kentucky Journalist Named Woman of the Year

"Carol Sutton, Ex-Managing Editor of C-J, Dies," *The Louisville Courier-Journal,* 20 February 1985.

"A Dozen Who Made A Difference." *Time Magazine* (January 5, 1976).

"Flight From Fluff." *Time Magazine* (March 20, 1972).

Harp, Dustin. "Newspapers Transition From Women's to Style Pages: What Were They Thinking?" *Association for Education in Journalism in Mass Communication,* http://list.msu.edu/cgi-bin/wa?A2=ind0310a&L=aejmc&F=&S=&P=9797.

Public Outcry Forces Closure of Maxey Flats

Cameron, Diane M., Barry D. Solomon and B. Cullingworth, eds. "Nuclear Waste Landscapes: How Permanent?" *Energy, Land & Public Policy-Environmental Policy.* New Brunswick: Transaction Publishers, 1990, pp. 137–86.

Denham, Mitchel. Legislative Research Commission. *Report of the Special Advisory Committee on Nuclear Waste Disposal No. 142.* Frankfort, 1977.

Donahue, Michael. *The Kentucky Encyclopedia.* Lexington, Ky.: University Press of Kentucky, 1993.

"Maxey Flats Superfund Proceeding Settled." *Educational Record* 77, no. 1 (Winter 1996).

Powell, Nancy. "A Concerned Community." *EPA Journal* 17, no. 3 (July/August 1991).

Worthington, Pete. Legislative Research Commission. *Report of the 1978–79 Interim Special Advisory Committee on Nuclear Waste Disposal No. 167.* Frankfort, 1980.

Operation BOPTROT

Cottle, Michelle. "Why Mitch McConnell Should Know Better." *Washington Monthly* 29, no. 10 (1997), pp. 9–14.

Drummond, Ayres, "With Leaders Leaving Office for Jail, Kentucky Works to Refurbish Image," *Special to the The New York Times, The New York Times* (1857–Current file). New York, N.Y.: 19 September 1993, p. 27

Mason, Bobbie Ann. "Doing the BOPTROT." *New Yorker Magazine* 70, no. 12 (1994), pp. 46–53.

Wilson, Richard and Tom Loftus, "First Legislator Indicted in Probe: Crupper to Quit and Plead Guilty to Taking Bribe," *The Louisville Courier-Journal,* 9 June 1992.

General

Kleber, John E. *The Encyclopedia of Louisville.* Lexington, KY.: University Press of Kentucky, 2001.

INDEX